SONG OF GOA

Mandos of Union and Lamentation

Song of Goa, no. 2

José Pereira, Micael Martins &
António da Costa

SONG OF GOA

Mandos of Union and Lamentation

ARYAN BOOKS INTERNATIONAL
NEW DELHI

SONG OF GOA, NO. 2

Mandos of Union and Lamentation

ISBN-81-7305-247-6 (HB)
ISBN-81-7305-248-4 (PB)

First Published in **2003** by :

ARYAN BOOKS INTERNATIONAL
Pooja Apts., 4B, Ansari Road, Darya Ganj New Delhi-2 (India)
Tel.: 23287589, 23255799; Fax: 91-11-23270385
E-mail: aryanbooks@vsnl.com

This work has been sponsored by

FUNDAÇÃO ORIENTE, GOA
ASMITAI PRATISTHAN

in conjunction with

GOLDEN HEART EMPORIUM, MARGÃO, GOA
SRINIVAS DEMPO
Chairman and Managing Director, Dempo Group

and

DATTARAJ V. SALGAOCAR
Managing Director, V.M. Salgaocar and Bro. Ltd.

Computer Typeset at ABI Prints & Publishing Co., New Delhi
Printed in India at B.B.N. Printers, New Delhi

THIS BOOK IS DEDICATED
TO THE THREE DAUGHTERS
OF MATEUS FRANCISCO PEREIRA (1875-1949)
AND LUCRÉCIA PACIÊNCIA MENEZES (1875-1951):

CARMELINA PEREIRA (1895-1969)
ANINHA PEREIRA E COSTA (1904-1988)
AND ESPECIALLY
ARSENTINA PEREIRA E COSTA (1907-1985),

WHO TAUGHT US TO LOVE AND ADMIRE
TRADITIONAL GOAN SONG
AND INSTRUCTED US IN THE SUBTLETIES OF THE MANDO

FIDELIUM DEUS
OMNIUM CONDITOR ET REDEMPTOR
ANIMABUS FAMULARUM TUARUM
REMISSIONEM CUNCTORUM TRIBUE PECCATORUM
UT INDULGENTIAM
QUAM SEMPER OPTAVERUNT
PIIS SUPPLICATIONIBUS CONSEQUANTUR

CONTENTS

TYPES AND SUBTYPES OF KONKANI SONG

I. RELIGIOUS SONGS
1. *Fugrhi* [1]
2. *God-dde Ramayann* [2]
3. *Launnim* [3]
4. Sacred art song, Christian [4]
5. Sacred art song, Hindu [5]
6. Sacred folk song, Christian [6]
7. Sacred folk song, Hindu [7]
8. *Zoti* [8]

II. CHILDHOOD SONGS
1. Child songs [9]
2. Childrens' songs [10]
3. *Duvallo* [11]
4. *Palnnam* [12]

III. MARRIAGE SONGS
1. Brahmin nuptial chants [13]
2. Kunnbi nuptial chants [14]
3. *Ovi/Vers/Zoti* [15]
4. Shudra/Sudir nuptial chants [16]
5. *Shobhane* [17]

IV. DEATH SONGS
1. *Banvarh* [18]
2. Dirges [19]

V. RANDOM FOLK SONGS [20]

VI. OCCUPATIONAL SONGS
1. Boat songs [21]
2. Street vendors' cries [22]
3. Work songs [23]

VII. CASTE SONGS OF THE GAURHOS, HARVIS & KUNNBIS
1. *Dhalo* [24]
2. Kunnbi songs [25]
3. *Talgarhi* [26]

VIII. THEATRICAL SONGS
1. *Fell* songs [27]
2. *Teatro* songs [28]
3. *Zagor* songs [29]
4. Story songs [30]

IX. DANCE SONGS, INCLUDING THE MANDO
1. *Deknni* [31]
2. *Dulpod* [32]
3. *Mando/Manddo* [33]
4. *Mando-dulpod* [34]

X. POPULAR ART SONGS [35]

Chapter 1

PROLOGUE

This volume is the second in a trilogy; the first, *Song of Goa. Mandos of Yearning*, was published by Aryan Books International in 2000. That volume has a lengthy Essay on the Mando, a general discourse on the types Konkani Song, a synopsis of Goan history, an overview of the evolution of Goan Song, and observations on the music, poetry and dance character of the Mando, the climax of Goan Song. That volume also contains appendices on the romanized spelling of Saxtti Konkani adopted in this book, and the manuscripts and informants on which our research is based.

1. THE MANDO: CLIMAX OF GOAN SONG

The cultural impact of the West on India was fertile, particularly in the fields of architecture and music. A whole tradition of song was continued or brought into being: the *monophonic*, of compositions of single melodic lines, controlled in time by rhythm, existent prior to the Western impact, but persisting after it; and the *harmonic*, of compositions simultaneously combining two or more notes into chords and relating the latter among themselves. To the two-dimensionality (melody-rhythm) of monophonic music, harmony added a third dimension, depth.

Unyielding in its individuality, the bi-millennial tradition of Indian classical music, founded on monophony, has a wide range of sophisticated instruments: of strings (like the *vina* and the *sitar*) and wind (*nagasvaram* and *shehnai*) for its melody, and of percussion (*mridanga* and *tabla*) for its rhythm. But its concerts involve small ensembles of not more than six musicians. In performance everything is related to the refinement of melodic line and the complexity of rhythm. The new musical tradition, of *harmony*, possessed of an ever-growing number of instruments, like the French horn, tuba, oboe, clarinet, bassoon, cello and violin (the latter adopted by Indian classical musicians), capable of being assembled into gigantic orchestras productive of epic configurations of architectonically organized sound like the symphony. There were also instruments ideal for solo performances, like the piano and organ (adopted by Goan musicians, but not by the Indian classical). The effect that this complex instrumentation can produce is heightened by its being combined with complex vocal performance, as that of a choir, where several voices are assigned to each part. By the 17th century, Goans had mastered Western choral music. In 1663, in Bom Jesus in Velha Goa, seven choirs sang an oratorio of the Baroque master GIACOMO CARISSIMI (1605-1674). Present at the performance was the Pope's legate, who felt that he was listening to a concert in Rome.

In the rest of the subcontinent, apart from the area of musical instruments (including the harmonium and the mandolin), Indian music absorbed little of the Western. Goan Song, for its part, also retained, to mark its rhythm, the *gumott*, a percussion instrument of traditional Indian provenance. It is shaped like a pot, of clay mixed with powdered glass to increase its resonance, and with a large and a small neck, each opposite the other. The large neck is covered with lizard skin, which is heated before it is struck, to make it properly taut. Goan harmonic music, basically Western in character, was nuanced by the use of grace notes, known in Konkani as *kongre* ("curved," "wavy," "curled"), an essential part of the melodic structure of

Indian music, as are the *gamakas,* or sound curves.

We can postulate that Goan Song has been in existence as long as its Konkani language, believed to have arisen around the 10th century. In its totality, monophonic and harmonic, the vocal music of Goa can be classified into the following ten categories, containing at least 35 identifiable types:

1. *Religious songs.* 8 types. Monophonic and harmonic
2. *Childhood songs.* 4 types. Monophonic
3. *Marriage songs.* 5 types. Monophonic and harmonic
4. *Death songs.* 2 types. Monophonic
5. *Random folk songs*
6. *Occupational songs.* 3 types. Monophonic
7. *Caste songs of the Gaurhos and Kunnbis.* 3 types. Monophonic and harmonic
8. *Theatrical songs.* 4 types. Monophonic and harmonic
9. *Dance songs, including the Mando.* 4 types. Harmonic
10. *Popular art songs.* Harmonic

The Mando, to be described below, is one of the four dance song types. The others that follow the Mando are, first, the *Deknni* ("Song of the Deccan" ?), sung in two-fourth time, imitating Hindu music in harmonic idiom, mostly descriptive of Hindu life, with focus on the temple dancers. Second, the *Dulpod,* in six-eight time, of quick rhythm, typically descriptive of everyday Goan life, especially that of the Christians. Third, the *Mando-Dulpod,* a quicker variety of the Mando, easing the transition from the latter to the faster Dulpod.

Two phenomena precipitated the rise of the Mando in the first half of the 19th century, the political events of the time and the introduction of social dancing into Goa.

Goan consciousness of politics was enkindled by the French Enlightenment, a movement, passionately devoted to freedom (but often brutal in realizing it), that urged a group of Goans to revolt against Portuguese authority and to try to set up a Goan republic, in the *Conjuração dos Pintos* (Conspiracy of the Pinto family, 5 August 1787). Part of their inspiration came from the words of a disciple of the Enlightenment, the Portuguese royal minister, the MARQUÊS DE POMBAL (1699-1782), in the service of king José (r. 1750-1777). In his edict of 1761, Pombal decreed that Asians and Europeans were to have the same legal and social status, since "His Majesty does not distinguish between his vassals by their colour but by their merits". But the colonial authorities, accustomed to treating their native subjects with contempt, baulked, so Pombal, in 1774, repeated that both Goans and Portuguese, outsiders and natives, were to be treated equally, since they were "equally the vassals of His Majesty," and that such equal treatment was "likewise conformable with divine, natural and human laws, which under no circumstances allow that outsiders should exclude the natives from the fruits of the soil where they were born, and the offices and benefices thereof".

Goan political consciousness was further inflamed by the establishment of a constitutional monarchy in Portugal, in 1820, in consequence of which elections were mandated in all the provinces of the Portuguese empire, including Goa. The natives made use of this opportunity to express their dislike of the colonial regime, always voting for candidates opposed to the government. Some of the earliest known mandos belong to this time, such as the one on the municipal election of the Ilhas district in 1854, which ended in the beating to death of the much hated mestizo Joaquim Garcêz and provoked savage government reprisals.

It was an age of turmoil, of which the elections were but one feature. Further exacerbation of the turmoil resulted from events like the British attempts to annex Goa (1799-1813); the ever-recurring revolts of the martial Rannos or hillmen of Sot-tori/Satari (as DIPU RANNO in 1822 and

KUXTTOBA in 1869); the involvement of Goan soldiers in the Portuguese colonial wars in Africa and their rebellion in 1870; and the great exodus of emigrants toward the end of the 19th century, facilitated by the introduction into Goa of the steamship (1870) and the railway (1886). The goal of the emigrants was, first, British India; next the British and Portuguese colonies around the Indian Ocean; and finally, in our days, Europe and the New World itself.

But the elections ushered in a new age of freedom for the Goans, and hastened the process of their westernization. Two centuries before Goans had become converts to Western civilization, at first unwillingly, but not long after, enthusiastically. They now believed that a more thorough acceptance of European cultural modes - but qualified always with Indian nuances and subject to Indian notions of propriety - would make them the complete equals of their arrogant colonial masters. They began to build mansions as grand as those of the latter, and to imitate more closely their dress and social habits (one of which was *social dancing*, in vogue in Goa from the 1830s). The dance became a craze in Goa's ballrooms; they were performed in their mansions' largest and most lavishly appointed halls. There was no type of dance that the Goans were not eager to learn, some of which had fallen out of fashion in Europe itself (like the Minuet and the Contredanse), but which Indian conservativeness kept alive in Goa. Others were the craze in Europe, like the Waltz, the Mazurka and the Polka.

In their dances the men (who had previously clothed themselves in white knee-length robes known as *kabạí*) now adopted the sombre-colored European suit, with its trousers and jacket, and sometimes vest. But the women retained their native two-piece *torhop-bazu* : the *torhop*, or sarong-like loin-cloth, and the *bazu* or bodice; covering both partly was the shawl (*tuvalo*). The distinctive piece is the *torhop*, a stylized version of the traditional Indian woman's loin-cloth, roughly 90 x 150cm. with two borders, each about 30cm. wide, one horizontal (along the lower edge of the cloth) and the other vertical (in the middle of the body), from the waist to the feet. In its ceremonial form, the *torhop-bazu*, known as the *fot*, was lined with bands of silk and velvet, and embroidered with ribands of gold thread.

Before the Mando originated, the most popular song type was the *Ovi* (or Vovi), originally a marriage song (category III), but also employed in hymns and for a variety of purposes — as to thank someone for favors, to reply to insults, and to express personal grief. The Ovi is a quatrain, as is the Mando's early form. But later, perhaps under the influence of the Portuguese Fado, a chorus was added to the quatrain, giving rise to the classical Mando, the climax of Goan Song.

Social dancing evolved in Europe from the 11th century, its main theme erotic passion or courtship. It appears to have originated in the courtly ideal of the Provençal troubadours and German Minnesingers ("singers of love"), and had three notes, *joi* (joy), *amor* (love) and *cortezia* (courtesy), the former two controlled by the latter. Previous to the application of *cortezia* love's various moods, from fervent passion to playful frolic, were allowed to surface wildly and wantonly, even to the point of sexual consummation. Interdicting such lusty displays, *cortezia* replaced them with a shy veneration for woman which, inflamed by music in the symmetry of movement, displayed itself in an airy proximity between the partners, where contact was subdued and dissimulated. As such, dances left an open space between couples; they were known as *open couple* dances. Indian ideas of propriety, in the (aristocratic) Mando, allowed only open couple dances. But sometimes defiant passion, as in the (bourgeois) Waltz, drew the couple into close embrace, giving rise to *close couple* dances. Open and close couple dances are only one of the dualities that qualify social dance.

Another duality can best be described in the words of

Sanskrit dance theorists, *tandava*, restless and even violent dance, expressed in leaps and leg thrusts; and *lasya*, balanced and graceful dance, performed in a "sweet manner" - or *douce manier*, in the language of the French Baroque dancing masters.

In the 16th century dance was moving toward the *lasya* mode, which triumphed in the age of the Baroque Minuet (or of LOUIS XIV, r. 1643-1715) and in that of the Rococo Contredanse (or of LOUIS XV, r. 1715-1774). The Mando can be represented as a kind of synthesis of these two dances.

We shall now describe the Mando in its three aspects, music, poetry and dance.

Music: The form of the Mando is binary (two stanzas, A + B, each repeated) and ternary (three stanzas, A + B + C, the first two forming the strophe and the last the chorus). Each stanza is sung in two voices and then repeated. In addition, a chorus of singers repeats the chorus. Mandos generally have three verses. The musical structure of the Mando is modulated with patterns making up phrases that follow one another in the same order. Rhythmically, the Mando consists of six beats (and is thus a simple sextuple), with two stresses, one on the first beat, and the other, the predominant stress, on the fifth. A mando generally opens on the fifth beat, but can open on any beat except the fourth. The Mando's time signature is six-four, with the crotchet or quarter note as its unit in time. Its tempo is usually *moderato*, M.M. = 96, but can move faster, between 106 and 120 to the beat.

The Mando is sung by a combination of two voices, the first voice singing the principal melody and the second the counterpoint. The second voice generally follows the first in parallel motion, in thirds and sixths, but is sometimes modulated with contrary motion. The singing is accompanied by the violin and the piano, chiefly for the melody, and by the *gumott*, to accentuate the rhythm.

Poetry: The language of the Mando is Konkani, in the Saxtti dialect as was spoken by the Brahmins of villages like Kurhtori/Curtorim, Lotlli/Loutulim and Rai/Raia (and is still, to a great extent, today). Saxtti is differentiated from the other Konkani dialects by its musicality and its exceptional and frequent use of elision. The metre is basically octosyllabic, divided into three feet, two anapaests and a trochee. The basic pattern can be abbreviated (through elision) or lengthened, as needed by the melody and the metre. The Mando's themes are basically four: *utrike*, the lovers' yearning for union; *ekvott*, the union achieved; *villap*, lament out of despair for union, or from other personal grief; and *fobro*, a narrative, frequently touched by malice, of events, domestic, local or political. The dominant emotion is melancholy; in the terms of Sanskrit aesthetics, the basic sentiment (*rasa*) is pathos (*karuna*). The words, on the other hand, convey imagery reflective of light and color: luminaries, jewels, flowers and angelic presences.

Among the Mando's many composers, the following may be mentioned: FREDERICO DE MELO (1834-1888) of Rai, LIGÓRIO COSTA (1851-1919) of Kurhtori, PAULO MILAGRES SILVA (1855-1931) of Lotlli, EDUARDO MENEZES (1862-1922) also of Lotlli, ARNALDO DE MENEZES (1863-1917) of Kurhtori, PASCOAL NORONHA (1872-1936) of Morhgoum/Margão, GIZELINO REBELO (1875-1931) of Vernnem/Verna, SEBASTIÃO COSTA-FERNANDES (1875-1948) of Kurhtori, and TORQUATO DE FIGUEIREDO (1875-1948) of Lotlli.

Dance: The Mando, India's *ballo nobile* (noble ballroom dance, fit for royalty), is an anachronistic synthesis of the two major dances of the 18th century, dances which represent the high point of the troubadour ideal of courtly love, the Minuet and the Contredanse.

The *Minuet* is a French open-couple dance in three-eight time, its movement close and minutely systematized. A dance of small steps, laden with etiquette and spectacularity, and involving choreographed figures or floor patterns, it is unsurpassed in its blend of dignity and charm, restrained sprightliness and aloof gallantry. It starts with the dancers making stylized and ceremonial bows and curtsies to the spectators. Then the gallant play of courtship and wooing begins. The sexes meet and separate gracefully, with dainty steps and glides, to the right and to the left, forwards and backwards, with quarter turns, approaching and retreating, searching and evading, now side by side, now touching hands, now facing, now gliding past one another, the women accenting the elegance of their motions by graceful movements of their (ostrich) fans. (The Mando was to adopt some of these features later.) In the Minuet, the erotic is so extremely stylized as to be almost unrecognizable.

Following the Minuet is the English *Contredanse,* a choral dance in two-four or six-eight time. It has two forms, the circle, where men and women alternate, and the double file, whey they face each other (as in the Mando). The underlying theme is love combat, with approach and retreat, separation and union. The Contredanse depends for its effect less on the elegance of bodily movements than on the smooth interweaving of figures and the harmonious cooperation of the couples. But for the partisans of the Minuet, devotees of minutely graceful motions, the Contredanse was no more than a tapping of feet and the tossing, twisting and turning of the body. Still, these supposedly ungraceful movements supplied constant occupation and pleasure to the spectator's eye through the variety of the arrangement of the lines of the dancers' bodies.

Many of these features were taken over by the Mando, with a restraint that Minuet lovers would have applauded. As we noted, the Mando is a kind of synthesis of Minuet and Contredanse. The drama of wooing and courtship is assumed from the latter, but the "tormenting of the body", attributed to the English Contredanse by the devotees of the Minuet, is replaced by the French dance's suave movements - those of the *lasya* or *douce manier*.

It was often in the evenings that the Mando dances took place, in the halls of the mansions that Goan aristocrats had been building from the 18th century. Crystal chandeliers were suspended from fretwork ceilings; porcelain of Chinese workmanship but of Indian design adorned tables of rosewood, whose polished black surfaces were carved with twining floral designs. The chandeliers were lit and filled the hall with "the lustre of stars and diamonds". From the vases on the tables and the window sills came "the perfume of jasmines and chrysanthemums".

A thump of the *gumott* would announce the start of the Mando dance. Two files of dancers would form, one of women, arrayed in *torhop-bazus* of silk and velvet, stiff with floral patterns in gold thread; and the other of men, in dark or gray suits, acting as a foil to the rich chroma of the file of the women. It was fashionable for the women to hold fans, as it had been in the Minuet, especially fans of ostrich feathers, so the women's file would become a long flutter of white.

In the expectant silence, the strains of the Mando, sad and solemn, would impel the files into motion, with movements of advance, the body now turning to the right, now to the left, now frontally positioned, now in three-quarters view. When almost face to face in the middle of the hall, the couples would retreat to their starting points, advance followed by recess, but with the same variation of figures. Sculptural poses would file before the spectators' eyes in unending silhouettes, some more grave, others more graceful. Another advance soon after, with the men and women gliding toward one another, the whole pattern of movement rounded off by a crossing and interchange of places.

The parts played by the men were actively passionate. Theirs were the moves of the chase, the making of ritual passes at the women. The movements of the women, on the other hand, were demure and modest, engaged in continually assumed attitudes of stylized wooing. With a sideward inclination of the head, half challenging, half shy, they would open their fans and let them fall lazily, hiding their faces behind the ostrich feathers in simulated bashfulness, as though to shield themselves from the mock-ardent glances of the men. These and other gesticulations signified ambush, invitation and refusal. Coyly toying a lock of hair and darting coquettish glances in the direction of their partners, they would continue the dialogue of courtship in the subtler language of the eyes.

It was as if Lady Cortezia, who had descended to earth in 11th-century Provence, was taking her leave in 19th century Goa, making her last curtseys and her last gestures of *joi* and *amor*.

The Mando flourished for a full century, from 1850 to 1950. A product of a tranquil feudal society, it was unable to withstand the turbulence produced by the large-scale emigration of the Goans from their homeland, as took place from the 19th century, and the collapse of the British and Portuguese empires in India. Today it survives as a caricature of its former self, beloved but betrayed.

2. THE ROMANTIC WORLD OF THE MANDO

The world of the Mando is a romantic world: it is preoccupied with love; it idealizes that emotion and its object, the beloved. The romanticism of this world can be portrayed, as we intend to do in this essay, through the words of the mandos themselves.

The Mando has a dual character; its two aspects exist in counterpoint. On the one hand, its *melody* is uniformly melancholic, suggesting the seriousness and even solemnity of the man-woman love relationship, and the tragedy that results when that relationship goes bad. For one mando, this relationship is almost religious and sacrificial in character, where the lover declares that he has dedicated his life to his beloved: "I erected an altar in my heart and offered the sacrifice of love". Thanking God for the depthless love that exists between herself and her lover, the inamorata affirms that only two beings exist for her, God in heaven and her lover on earth.

On the other hand, in contrast to the melancholy, the *text* is suffused with the imagery of light. Constant reference is made to the stars, the chief of which is the sun, as well as to its satellite the moon. "The sky of those days of our joy," exclaims the young man parting forever from his girl, "is transparent and clear. There is no end to the stars" (*Sorgu nitoll go nirmollu Te amcha sukach' go disantso Xevott nam go noketrantso*, FREDERICO DE MELO, 1834-1888)! But the physical light of sun, moon and stars is only an analogue of the holy light of heaven, a light especially reflected in heaven's ministers, the angels. "As you are an angel of heaven, the light of the stars has dawned... The light of heaven descended upon us; it was a light destined for us by God... We received our (marriage) sacrament today, in the light of the saints and the blessed".

Our analysis of the Mando's content can be divided into three sections. *First*, love, leading to union, sacramentally solemnized in marriage. *Second*, the factors in the daily life of the lovers that usually frustrate that union. And *third*, the tragic breakdown of union, ending in separation, with its sad consequences.

I. Love Leading to Union

Love begins to affect the sexes when they are very young, even when they are in school. A schoolboy, not yet 17, is obsessed with his girl, Maria, and drops his studies (*Mariecha lagunum mogako Estudako lailo tannem uzo*). A young man remembers the day when he first saw his beloved: it was on the first of March; the sight of her angelic face revealed to him what love was. "The moment I saw you, I felt that it was wonderful to live" (*Tuka dektrich tedech vella Sonsar zai-i zalo maka,* ARNALDO DE MENEZES, 1863-1917). Fired by their newly found friendship, the lovers yearn to always be in each other's company. They exclaim: "How can I ever live without your loving heart? ... Without seeing you, I cannot live through a single day... If I do not see you at least once every day, my mind almost goes mad!" They can enjoy each other's company in tranquil security only when protected by the inviolable institution of holy matrimony, when the loving friends will be "united by the Holy Spirit".

Still, marriage is no infallible recipe for happiness; it is pain for the daughters but life for the sons (*dizgras tsolianchem vido tsoleanchem*). Union with the lovely lady would seem to be the very acme of bliss. The rapturous wooer can find no words to describe his sweetheart's loveliness. His portrait of her is filled with metaphors of light and allusions to those beings of light, the angels. Lover and beloved are connected like star and starlight; their companionship is like that of angels. The beloved is "an angel of lovely form...an angel of heaven, radiating starlight". She has "the clear and spotless face of an angel". Your "angel face," declares the lover, "is engraved in my heart". She "shines like the sun and stars" (*Surya noketranche porim porzolleta,* GIZELINO REBELO, 1875-1931). She is the "star of the morning" (*Estrel faleavelem,* INÁCIO FERNANDES, 1872-1927), a star that beams in the lover's bosom, a star that has "flown down from heaven... You, lady, are the light of the stars". The sweetheart is also compared to the moon; indeed, she is the very "loveliness of the moon" (*sundorai-i tsondrimanchi,* ANTÓNIO JOÃO DIAS, 1857-1931), of a moon that dawns in the impassioned admirer's heart. A more frequent comparison is with the sun. The lady's face is "more splendid than the sun," which too arises in the young man's heart. The bride's innocent life is "purer and more spotless than the sun". Light images not derived from the heavenly bodies are less frequent: the lady is a lamp to the lover's eyes, a powerful lighthouse flash. However, she is often described in terms of a mineral that reflects light - a jewel or gem. When she abandons her lover, she can be compared to a jewel that, all of a sudden, flies away from his bosom like an eagle... "steeping my soul and body in sorrow". Occasionally, her person is said to combine beauty and holiness, for she is "a reliquary of gems and pearls". Constant and faithful love between husband and wife is compared to a diamond.

Of the images that make no reference to light, the most common are those of flowers, blooms of luminous color. The enraptured wooer exclaims: "Beautiful flower that you are, I adore you... A flower of perfume you are, the rose of Jericho". The love-lorn girl, her desires unfulfilled, is a "drooping flower," but the poet promises to refresh her with his "sprinkling". The thought of the lady evokes floral images. "When I take you in my arms, I breathe the perfume of rosemaries... When the jasmine bush puts forth buds, I gaze at the flowers... When the thought of you comes to me, I smell the perfume of jasmines... Love, my love, [I inhale] lavender perfumes!" A young man, meeting a girl on the road, declares his love for her by asking her for the flowers she has in her hand. Occasionally stars are compared to flowers, as when describing a parting: "This star of the morning [the lady-love] faded away like a chrysanthemum".

As for the young man's looks, the Mando does not pause long over them, except sometimes to mention that he has an angel face and curly hair. To his girl, his looks seem to matter less than his dress; his stylish attire sets her heart a-flutter. Young men, for their part, try to impress a pretty girl by parting their hair in modish ways (*Vankrhe-tinkrhe kortai mage).*

Coming down to details, the Mando's description of the inamorata focuses on her face, which is jewel-like in appearance, and as beautiful as a star. Her cheeks are red roses, amber, clusters of jasmine buds and pearls. She has ivory teeth and a dazzling smile. Her lips are red roses, or are pale orange, the color of that typically Goan flower, the *abolem* (*crossandra undulaefolia*). But the beauty of her face is concentrated on her eyes, which Brahmin youths come from everywhere especially to admire (*Te tuj' dolleanko tsoichak go Yetai bambnnale tsole,* LIGÓRIO COSTA, 1851-1919). Little attention is given to the rest of her body, as for instance, her hands, pictured as being rounded, like the work of a turner.

Overwhelmed by her beauty and grace, the gallant addresses his darling as "angel", and in phrases like "my love, love of my love, love of my inner being, my heart [or, my heart-cluster, *kallizatso gonddu*], my jewel". The lady addresses her beau in much the same way, as "love, love of my love, my angel, my archangel".

In the world of the Mando, the wish of the parents was law. Before they wed, the lovers found it hard to meet. They had to show signs of their love from some distance, such as the lady sending her admirer a flower, or undoing her coil of hair and letting it fall on her shoulder (an act also indicative of sorrow). But the most powerful sign was the language of the eyes. "Caress me with loving eyes" (*Mogache dolle lai re maka,* EDUARDO MENEZES, 1862-1922). The impassioned maiden shows her infatuation for her admirer by her strange behavior. She talks and laughs endlessly in church, pretends to be reading her missal, turning this page and that; at the end of the mass she makes a show of greeting every one outside. At home she throws herself on her bed, and talks of intimate family matters with all and sundry. "You must not worry about this, love," the composer makes her say; "I often get many such moods" (*Osoly' sintment zaite zatai maka*). As for the man, the sign he gives her is a picture of himself, in response to the lady's uncoiling of her hair.

So where and when do the lovers meet? In front of the inamorata's window, on moonlit nights, on the way to church, when bathing at springs, at the seaside, at weddings, and also at the Carnival and during the days of Lent. Regular meetings at home are allowed only when the couple is engaged or if kind parents permit. Fortunate is the man who is the girl's tutor (when he can prematurely and furtively make love to her!), but clandestine encounters at her home are possible when her parents are away.

A good place to meet is at the girl's *window*, where she is sometimes seen playing the viola, gazing in the mirror and showing herself. "I sit at the window and comb my hair, waiting for my friend... watching for his shadow," reports she. "Why do you sit at the window," queries her unhappy boyfriend, "and shed so many tears?"

Moonlit nights are a good time to meet, especially when there are no prying eyes. It was on one wonderful night, exclaims the lover, "that the lovely princess, of beautiful form, came into my arms!" A poet says to his lady, "I saw you, my love, in the light of the moon, standing at the door of your porch".

There can be frequent encounters on the way to (or in) *church*, but no close contact. In church, says the young man, "I keep looking for you on Sunday. When you appear, I am filled with joy... my eyes blink". But conversation may not be easy. When in the presence of his lady, the ardent lover is all a-flutter (*sogloch usrumuttetalo*). So total is his devotion to her that he even dedicates the mass he hears to her (*misso dekun tika bettoitalo*). But the lovers have no privacy. "I cannot find a single day to tell you love's secrets". Not all these encounters are joyful, however. "On my way to church on Sundays," moans the rejected suitor, "I used to moisten my kerchief with perfume, as I do now with tears".

Bathing at springs, alone or in company with other men or women, was a permitted custom. "When I think of the baths we had together... our clean and pure baths," says the lover, "my heart is on fire". When that fire heats up, the lover may have to bathe alone, to cool his ardor: "I cannot bear it, love, I feel like bathing in the Rumborhdem spring" (*To sonsum' nuzo moga Rumbrhech' zorits' banhu ge-in dista*, SEBASTIÃO COSTA-FERNANDES, 1875-1937). The lovers may also run into each other at the *seaside*, where it is the custom for families to go during the hot months preceding the monsoon, to picnic, to enjoy the fresh air, and to bathe.

Lovers could meet, talk and even dance at *weddings*, which, alas, were not a daily occurrence. "When we go in the evening to the wedding, let us both dance the Contredanse... Taking our friends for company, let us sing a mando".

During the *Carnival*, the three days of fun preceding the penitential season of Lent, lovers had greater freedom to converse and to declare their love, to deepen their intimacy or to end it: "On that Carnival day, do you remember what you told me? It was then that I found out you loved me... On that Carnival day, my love seems to have gone mad. Why, coming at midnight, did you knock on my window? ... During the whole of *Lent* you made my heart suffocate. You were angry at me, you scowled; why are you turning your back on me," complains a rejected suitor.

However, it is at the *lady's home* that the most intriguing trysts are made, furtively, when her parents are away. "Looking out for the time when no one is around, I will embrace you," says the lover. "Go," cries the girl, "dad will be home soon!" Boy: "Do not cry, my dear, I'll never leave you!" Rarely, the meeting lasts a whole night. "My love," declares the ardent courtier, "I will come in the evening and say good-bye, my jewel, in the morning!" But other admirers are not so successful: "The whole village ward is full of reports that you wander about at night. If you come to our house, father will kick you out!" Of course, all meetings between lovers are right and proper once they are engaged: "Tell me now, lady-love, see if you can come to our home".

Having decided that they cannot live without each other, and therefore, to wed, they plight their troth. The lady swears an oath before the man she loves, "by the wave of the sea, by the stars of heaven, by my tress of hair". The man says: "I swear to you that I want none but you... Do not be stricken by the curse of my suffering (*birmoty*). I give you my solemn promise to marry you". The lovers declare that they are exclusively devoted to each other. "I forsake all my friends and cleave to you alone, for you divined the secrets of my heart... I give you my word that I have no one but you". Happiness for them is not possible except in each other's company. "How can I ever live without your lovely heart? With my whole being I implore God for our union... I cannot, O I cannot, face life without you!" The couple hopes that their love will never die. "I pray God that you may foster this love," says the betrothed to her suitor, "Do not forget the love of love... Let us always keep this trust and never lose this affection. Let us remain always one". The commitment of the beloved to the lover is total; she cares more for his happiness than for her own. "My angel, if I die, may you find happiness after me. But if you die - may that day never dawn for me". To renege on this commitment, and the oath that solemnizes it, is the supreme disgrace.

What do the lovers do when not in each other's company? They gaze at the stars, indulge in music and song, look yearningly at each other's portraits, write letters, and meet in dreams. Absence is particularly painful during the dull, dark and wet days of the rainy season. "With the dismal monotonous patter of the rain [*bim, bim, pausu pottta*] outside, my lonely heart smarts with grief! Now unless I see you, I have no joy".

Memories of the lover arise during the evening: "You

used to visit me in the evenings [for three hours], now without you the three hours seem like three years". Night is the special time for tender memories: "All night my eyes burn... The thought of your virtues comes to me at night... I get the fever of love at night. "

When the memories arise, the lovers distract themselves by *gazing at the stars and heavenly bodies*. "When I look at the moon, my precious, I shed tears weeping for you... While the thought of you comes, I while away my time gazing at the stars (*Tuzo ugrhas yetrich moga Noketranchery vellu passar kortam*, FRANCISCO SARDINHA, 1897-1958)... In the evening I go for a walk and put my trust in the stars... Even the stars weep for me; forming letters by themselves, they show me your name... Moon, sun, stars, do not abandon me and go away!"

Another distraction is *indulging in music and song*. The doleful swain exclaims: "I sit on my porch and sing our song, crying with floods of tears, wondering if I should ever see you again". The lady says: "When the flute is played, memories of you come to me... I wear a red dress and play our song on the piano. Thinking of your virtues, I let my tears fall on the piano".

The pain of separation is somewhat alleviated by *looking at the lover's portrait*. "I take my viola in my hand and gaze at your portrait... Your likeness flashes before my eyes... I have kept the painted portrait of you in my heart... Fixing my eyes on your likeness, I wet my pillow with my tears... Make a parcel of your picture and send it to me. I will pass the rest of my days looking at your likeness" (*Urloly' dis karhtam sarkea' tuja tsoinum*, MARIANO COSTA, 1898-1931).

One can keep in touch with one's absent partner through *letters*. "I spend many nights reading your letters where you swear to be true to me... I send you letters always, because you have gone home. I often go to the post office, hoping a reply will come... When no letter comes, I become pensive. O love, what has happened to you, do write and tell me! ... Do not forget my love. I will write to you every week. Dear husband, send me news of yourself".

But union with an absent lover can take place in *dreams*. "If you do not come for a single day, I see you in my dreams... When I see you in my dreams, I embrace and kiss you... I saw you in my dream, and you woke me up with stabs of anguish! ... On one night, when I was asleep, my precious one, I took you in my arms; it seemed as if the sun had risen in the clouds! ... Good-bye, my angel, good-bye. In my dreams, at least, appear to me".

All uncertainty and pain end, and yearning finds fulfillment, in the marriage *union*, with the *rising sun* being the herald of the auspicious wedding day. "The sun arose in joy; the stars formed a circle around it... The light beams with the sun. The splendor of the stars has paled". But the physical sunrise symbolizes an inner dawn: "A blaze of light shone of a sudden", exclaims the ecstatic bride-to-be, "and the sun arose in my heart".

But it is in the evening, at the hour of *sunset,* that the main marriage celebrations begin. "The sun has extinguished its light, the splendor of the stars flashes forth... The moon has risen; the [setting] sun has beamed its rays... The moon shone in the clouds. The light of the sun was hidden... Today there is a tumult of stars, a ding-dong of bells (*gonngonnu re ganttantso*)... Today is the day of happiness. In heaven there is the light of stars. We received the sacrament of our own free will, in the light of heaven".

Light shines not only in heaven, but in the *marriage hall* too, which is adorned with lamps and flowers. "There is everywhere the perfume of jasmines and the strong aroma of champaks... Our house glows with light. The perfume of the jasmines - may God ever preserve it! "

The day of the wedding is especially the *bride* 's day, when she sings the marriage mando, and pours out her love for her groom. "Angel of my future emblazoned with stars

(*Noketranim surngailolea Muja furharacha anja*)! My parents chose you and God destined you for me... I cherished your sacred promise in my heart. Storms and tempests came, and misfortunes too, but we never wavered. I put my trust in your words and waited in hope. Because you are good I came into your arms, and now am happy... I have surrendered my maiden life and sought you out on this day... For you I sacrifice my unsullied life... I offer you my pure life; for this our destiny was determined in heaven... I saved my whole life for you. The word we spoke with our eyes let us forever keep it in our minds (*Dolleany'm sangyloly'm utor amchem Sodanch monantum dovorchem*)... Joy surges in my heart. I breathe a sigh of affection, and kiss you on the mouth. Let us live in love, you and me... Come, O come to me, love. I yearn for you. I have sought love's companionship: may God make it eternal... I felt the need for company, and to be mistress of this house... We are not strangers to each other, but like two fruits growing on the same tree... [We need each other, for] even a pestle of gold needs the support of the mortar wall" (*Bangrach' daie adar unttitso,* PASCOAL NORONHA, 1872-1936).

Though the bride is the queen of the wedding day, the king, that is, the *bridegroom,* does not remain wholly silent: "The days of our single life are at an end for me. God has forever extinguished out hearts' sighs... If you give me your true word, I will wear out my hands and feet and make you happy" (*Forench utor dileary maka At-paim' zoroin feliz kortol'm tuka*).

The union of the two lovers is sanctified by the *sacrament.* "Our family wishing it, the Church has united us... Our sacred union has become real. In the union of the sacrament, we have both been filled with grace... Our sacrament, predestined by yearning, we have today fulfilled in union... Our hearts have been made one today by the end of the stole... In the light of the saints and the blessed we have received the sacrament. May the sacrament of union become one of light... May our sacrament be one of God's blessing... Loving each other we will watch over our marriage sacrament... The married state is ever a sacrament adorned with gold. Created by God's love, it was destined for us today... The holy water and God's minister [the priest] gave us strength".

Even a day as blissful as the wedding day, is not devoid of *pain* - the pain of the bride at being separated from her family. "I have emerged today from father's and mother's sheltering care. The thought of this brought tears to my eyes. From today, I will belong to my husband's family"... But the start of wedded bliss may make one forgetful. "Do not," the bridegroom is reminded, "because you are married, forget your brethren". There is also the memory of the trials that preceded the marriage, trials which, if not overcome, would have wrecked all chances of the marriage ever taking place. "Ours is a sacrament of trials. May God now make it joyful". Without much effort and many reverses, the wedding day would never have dawned. "To marry you, I wrecked the world and put it together again".

But all pain is drowned in blissful thoughts of the *future,* and the need to preserve the bliss when inevitably problems will arise. "We must watch over this union like angels... Our life, let us offer it to God alone... Let us thank God, so we can obtain happiness and joy... Ending our virginal life, let us keep to the way of grace... Let us pray that we may always live in happiness... May heaven's blessing descend upon us, and may we always move in joy... May we happily pass our days in each other's company... We must face the future by doing good and trusting in God. I ask for your help in life, and I will always give you mine". The Mando is truly a Romantic song, for the happiness of marriage is thought of in terms of the couple only; there is no anticipation of the joy of children. And what happens when tensions arise in this blissful relationship? "If trouble comes to us through our own fault, let us not blame others for it... Though storms come upon us, love, I will never desert you".

After their wedding, the lovers, expected to be virginal up to that moment, can indulge in *passionate sex*. Exclaims the bride: "Love, come. My love, do come. I cannot wait. Love's fire burns" (*Moga yo Moga yo tum yo Mujan ravum' nuzo Mogan maryta uzo,* ALEIXO ANTÓNIO COSTA, 1874-1936)!

However, even though the Mando composers severely disapprove, man and woman will come together in sexual congress even without the benefit of sacrament. "I am married in Goa. I have a wife by virtue of the sacrament (*Bail muji sacramentachi).* And I have kept one in Bombay - for my diversion" (*Eki dovol-lea divertimentachi).* There will always be promiscuous women: "Do not put on an angelic face. I recognized you in the wedding hall. Show a candle to all men. Make a hundred friends, make sixty" (*Amig kory tum xembory satti*)! Some of these friends are wonderful in bed: "When I have such a friend, I never even think of my husband!" These men attend to their partners' erotic cravings in secret: "Watching for the time when there is nobody around, I embrace you... Satisfy me, at the time when there is no one near... After you there won't be anyone, my darling, to give me love's embrace". Loss of virginity before marriage is decried. A girl had relations with many men. "Finally this wilted flower fell to the lot of Noronh bab!" However, such casual contacts often end in disgrace. A woman has a number of paramours, but her extreme promiscuity annoys them. "However coquettishly you may act, you wench, no one will take any notice of you. Your unfaithfulness has made me jilt you. Nobody can want a hell such as you! How many children are you a mother of? Why pretend you are a virgin?"

A problem that concerned the day of the wedding was the bride's *attire*. While the men wore Western clothes, the

Brahmin women retained the Goan *torhop* (a sarong-like loin-cloth) and *bazu* (bodice). Yet some women were adopting the Western frock; a bridegroom is reported to be insisting on his bride marrying in that dress. But another bride says: "I very much wanted to be wed in *bazu-torhop.* My father had no wish to have me married in a frock".

Finally, there was the question of *caste*. The Mando is concerned mostly with Brahmin marriages, and only rarely, and unsympathetically, refers to inter-caste unions. One mando speaks of one such wedding, where the bride, not without a touch of irony, says: "I was always set against marrying outside caste. Father and mother insisted, because, they said, I would get heaps of money. I know now, after some thinking, that God created Adam alone. He made no Shudras, Chardos or Brahmins. All that is the falsehood of the world. Let us put caste aside. Take me to love's pleasures at once" (*Castam amim galya re poro Mogach' sukak vegim maka voro*, JOAQUIM SANTANA MENEZES, 1898-1939)!

II. Factors Connected with Union and Separation

But union can be frustrated, though not rendered impossible, by factors like dowry, malicious gossip of anonymous individuals, the intrigues of a personal enemy, and the emigration of a lover to a distant land. When overcome, however, they assure the success of the union. *Dowry* is the money, goods, or estate that the wife brings to her husband at marriage. It was presumably intended as the father's means of support of his daughter when she was no longer in his care. In the world of the Mando, marriage was inconceivable without dowry, and the inability of parents to pay it in the quantity demanded, or at all, often led to the tragic separation of the lovers.

The prospective bridegroom's spectrum of feelings about dowry is reflected in the following statements: "Ask your mother. See how much dowry they will give me... O, the dowry is little, and the presents not enough... I have put the engagement ring on you. I will count the dowry first... Your father cannot give a dowry for the kind of husband you seek... Even though the dowry be little, I will marry you... No matter how many thousands [of rupees] I get, I will never renounce you!" The lady, for her part, says: "Mother and father, of my portion of the inheritance, make a deed of dowry and give it to me..." Though I have much wealth, father kept me at home. Love, do not you worry about dowry. Our lands furnish enough for my share; its value will be around five thousand [rupees]... They say the dowry is little. The girl is so beautiful. O, marry me please with my elder brother's [financial] help!" A defiant girl marries with no dowry at all; she exclaims: "I have married. Dad, do not give your thousands!"

Another destroyer of the bond between lovers was the malicious *gossip* of people envious of the joy and harmony created by that bond. Underhanded intrigue and tale bearing would create discord between the loving couple, particularly if they wished to keep their courtship secret: "We kept our union secret; now the whole world has heard of it... I have no way of showing you my love. People prowl around looking for a chance to gossip about you and me... Enemies rage loudly outside, seeing our union. The fiends are at large, seeking to destroy our friendship!" The gossip would insinuate (if not openly declare) that the relationship was a promiscuous one. In all cases, the lovers would protest that their love was pure and chaste; indeed, angelic. But some love relationships were not only unaffected but even strengthened by that gossip. "People are envious because we are happy in love. Let people say what they like. Let us not lose our friendship... Even though our enemies shout, let us get together some day... Our four-month love was a love of innocent hearts. It was watered by people's gossip. God kept it pure... Our love was not furtive. It was angelically pure". But, all too often, gossip produced its deadly effects, and tore the lovers apart. The innocent party expresses its futile indignation. "Why are you moved by the malice of the blind? Why do you scowl? (*tonddo kallem kornum*)... We lived happily in loving companionship. How can you have changed, listening to people's gossip? ... Our friendship was ruined... Involved in a scandal [says the lady] I became desperate... Because of people's talk, you were hurt. That is why you must not have spoken to me on our way to mass... Do not turn your back on me. Do not listen to another's talk!"

Besides anonymous gossipers, an individual, usually a man, the lover's rival or *enemy*, comes between the lovers, and sunders them, often by replacing himself in the lady's affections. The betrayed lover implores his beloved not to listen to his rival. "An enemy came between us, and sundered our love. There was only one enemy, lady, and he was in your arms! ... Why are you cruel and ungrateful? An enemy is out to deceive you... Listening to the advice of the enemy, do not forget our love". Sometimes the enemy's name is mentioned: "I put my trust in love; Jacques Estibeiro betrayed us! ... Shame, shame on you, César Pinho! What have you done? Was it you who betrayed me? ... I call down seven curses on the man who betrayed me!" But the injured party can appear to be forgiving: "I say good-bye to you: may the man who betrayed us prosper!"

At times the relationship breaks up because of the *emigration* of the lover to a far-off land, because he is unhappy in Goa, and wants to seek a new life. He may have lost interest in his lady-love, in which case the break-up is permanent; or he may promise to come back to her when he has made his fortune. "This is a land of misfortune. I have now to look for a secure life. I can only stifle the love in my heart and leave Goa... Love of my happiness, why are you turning your back on me? What offended you that you should leave me and go to Damão? ... We enjoyed our company for a little while. Suddenly, you left for Bombay and betrayed me... You are leaving your friends and going in search of fortune. I wait with yearning to see your happiness... You are beyond the seven seas, and I yearn to see you. But I do not have father's permission to go... When you go to Portugal, who will give me news of you?" [The lover replies] "... I'll come back when I am rich and make you my wife". But the lady may herself go and join her man. "When you go abroad, do not let me continue to be lonely. Find a way, so that I can join you". Strangely enough, the parting can have an unearthly quality about it: "The time of our parting seemed that of the angels of heaven!" It is more natural, however, for the parting to produce a deep sadness: "The moment of farewell approaches. O, my heart suffocates! At the time of farewell, I lose all hope in life. Go, go dear, and do not cry! God will make you happy" (*Adeus kortso vellu pauta Ai mujem kallizo fapsota Dispidiro korcha vella O sonsar bongum maka dista. Voso vos re rorhum naka Deu-u feliz kortol' tuka*, TORQUATO DE FIGUEIREDO, 1876-1948)!

III. Final Separation of Lovers and Consequences

The four factors described frequently work against the lovers, and they cannot marry. Their suffering makes them despair: "The destiny of us both is to live in singleness. This is not the fault of father and mother, but only of the day of our birth".

But it often is the fault of father and mother, of *unsympathetic parents*: "Papa and mama do not want to marry me to you. Let us pray that they may come to understand, and that our destiny may be blessed... Because papa and mama are obdurate, they are killing me through suffocation". It is the *father* who is mainly to blame. "Because of your father, my love, I am giving you up and going away... My father did not wish me to marry you. My mind nearly went mad. It was as if a rock had fallen on my heart! ... I trample the hills of Bod-ddem [says the son, who describes himself as 'demon-struck'], because my father is not thinking of marrying me... My father despised me, and so I have remained unwed to this day... We conducted our courtship in secret, but father betrayed us... Father became crazed at the time of our happiness. Because he is false, he made me cry... Do not do it father [cries the despairing son], do not do what you did in October!" Understandably, the son wishes his father were dead, and even exults when he in fact dies: "God, save his soul at least, and take him to heaven!" He even brings himself to say, "My accursed father has died" (*Papa melo re bonglelo*)!

A mother can be unsympathetic too. "My mother is cruel by nature. I cry because of her hard-heartedness!" One such mother actually seems to enjoy tormenting her daughter: "No, no, no and no! I will not marry you! There is no hell on earth like you!" Of course, not all parents are of this sort; the number of Union mandos suggests that most placed the happiness of their children above all else. One such kind mother is affectionately remembered: "Because mother has a soft heart, she agreed to all that we asked for". *Relatives* can be unsympathetic too. "Because you are courting me, your in-laws are angry. Let whatever is to happen, happen, but let us fulfill our promise".

Sometimes the lovers' misfortunes are blamed not on the parents but on the cruel stars and on *fate*. "[In the days of our happiness] the stars of heaven were resplendent. Now look at them, love. They appear cruel... Reflecting on my future, I weep for the day I was born, for the portent of that moment and for the malignant stars! ... I get up in the morning, and sit and cry about the time of my birth... Mother, what an inauspicious moment was the time when I was born!"

But the most hurtful cause of the break-up is *betrayal*. Fidelity is compared to gold and faithlessness to copper.

Betrayal is described as melting gold. The exclamations of the betrayed are heartbreaking: "You came as an angel and became a demon... Cruel and perfidious friend, who created you in this world? Your first promise of love penetrated my heart. How could you bring yourself to leave me and go away? ... You scoundrel, for love of you I rejected all other suitors! ... I never believed that you would be false to me. I have no wish to live, and say my last good-bye to you". As often happens, betrayal results from affection being transferred to a third person. "Because you are an ingrate you have met someone else". Sometimes the mendacity of the betrayer is in evidence while he is still courting the person he is to betray: "You used to play false with me, and ask for my pardon on your knees. I forgave you for God's sake. From that day, I broke our engagement". Yet, not seldom, the break-up takes place because the loved person was not what he or she seemed: "I want none of you! I found out that you were bad! No one wants a hell like you!"

Betrayed lovers acutely feel the *pain of separation:* its sharpness is compared to transfixion by arrows and piercing by swords (the latter an allusion to Luke 2: 35, where Simeon tells the Madonna, "A sword shall pierce your heart!" Mary's heart is shown as being transfixed by seven swords): "I never believed that you would abandon me so soon, after piercing my heart with arrows upon arrows... What did I do to you, that you should leave me after transfixing me with one arrow after another! ... The misery and sorrow you have caused me do not leave my mind, Marianinha... Seven swords stabbed my heart, Marianinha, and we parted... I have been tormented, Marianinha, both body and soul. All this pain, Marianinha, I bore to no purpose at all".

Separation becomes more painful when accompanied by *abandonment by friends*. "If I search the whole world, I can find none. My friends have left me and gone away...

Hard-hearted friends," exclaims a mistress rejected by her paramours, "Why are you deserting me?"

Though the break-up has taken place, the lovers wish it had not; despair is replaced or accompanied by *futile yearning*. "Agonies afflict my heart because you have gone, leaving me alone... Your loving embraces come up before my eyes... I even begged you on my knees not to forsake me... How can I let go the jewel of my bosom! ... My sensitive heart's wounds reopen again... I weep with floods of tears. My life knows no peace... I cannot finish speaking of the agony in my heart. Seething blasts of heat, one upon another, have melted it, O God!" It is an agony that only God can understand: "O, the torments of my body! O, may God relieve me of them! ... O, my floods of tears - only God can understand them! ... The agonies and heartbreaks of life - to whom, Lord, shall I tell about them? ... At least you, Lord, listen to the sigh of my heart!" In spite of futile yearning, the lover may be forgiving: "Good-bye, my jewel, good-bye! I bid you farewell. Be happy, at least, and show yourself to me... Angel, when you are married, never forget to think of me".

Other lovers, however, are not so forgiving, but *curse* the betrayer: "May the heartaches you made me endure become yours too... When the wedding bells ring, my curses will stick to you!" The curse of the innocent sufferer is believed to infect the unjust cause of that suffering; this curse is described by that typically Konkani word *birmoty*. "You are trying to turn your back on me. The curse of my suffering will infect you! ... Let the curse of my suffering infect you, because you betrayed me (*Muji birmoty funttum tuka Trair tunvem kelo dekun maka)*... Let the man who betrayed me be stricken with the curse of my suffering... because he ruined my life!"

Unwilling ever to part, the ardent lover yearns for a *final embrace*. "Go, if you must, dear, when you have given me one last embrace... If there is no other way, give me one last embrace... A terrible time has come upon us, the time to say good-bye. Let us seek the company of the stars. Come, my love, give me one last embrace of happiness!" This is the final farewell: "When we were young we gave our promise of love. We have now fulfilled it [says the lover sarcastically]. So let us now end it... Love, come, my friend, come. Give me one last hug of joy! ... Standing at the chapel door, I spoke to you for the last time".

But the despairing love, futilely yearning, is attended by a *death wish*. You betrayed me; so pray for my quick death... My father and mother died, leaving me helpless. Mother, pray to God that I may die soon... When my eyes will shut, my love, my last sigh will be for you... Accept my embrace, love, and pray that I may die in peace... May God make you happy. As for me, let me fall by the wayside and die! ... I say good-bye, my love, and good-bye. I will put you out of my mind. I will hide myself in the grave... When I become dust, my love, do not shed copious tears... When my eyes shut, my darling, do not shed tears afterwards. When you have buried me in a grave, do not sit on the grave and cry... When you dig up my grave and look, you will find only bones". Sometimes the love-smitten man or woman do not wait for death, and threaten *suicide*: "If you leave me and go, my angel, I will give up my life for you... If you turn your back on me, I'll give up my life for your sake!"

But love, fulfilled or betrayed, can outlive the tomb: "Your memory will be my companion even when I become dust" (*Tuzo ugrhas mak' sangati Zaleary pasunum muji mati*, PAULO MILAGRES SILVA, 1855-1931).

For the aspiring lover, union with the beloved, when still believed possible, was the very height of happiness: "When I thought of your charm, the world seemed the very bliss of heaven!" But now, all hope of attaining that (mortal) bliss having vanished, the thoughts of the lover turn to (the immortal bliss of) *heaven*. Says a mother, unable to get her daughter wed: "What shall I do, my daughter? God is great for us. If we keep our trust in Him, He will give us heaven... Friend [says the lover to the betrayer], at least pray to God that when I die I will attain the joy of heaven". God's mercy and the lover's penitence are the road to heaven. "At least you, Lord, have pity on me and take me to your kingdom... We must live in misery [says the frustrated poet, speaking ironically], and reach the gate of heaven. We must ponder the lives of the saints and ask that we die soon... Asking forgiveness for our sins, we must climb up to heaven". A final good-bye, and then the sufferer is in heaven forever, in the company of angels. "Saying good-bye to all, I climb the stairs of heaven... O my heavenly angels take me to your bosoms. Safeguarding my soul, accompany me to heaven... O my angel of heaven, do not leave me and go away! ... I have turned my back on the world. Take me to the company of the angels".

These lovers seek heaven as a solace for their personal pain, where they will presumably be free from the company of their betrayers. But other lovers think of heaven as a place of reunion with those whom they loved, even those who betrayed them. "How can I say good-bye and leave you? Let us at least come together when we die... May our union become real at least after we die... I have lost all joy in life, my dear one. In heaven at least, speak a word to me! ... Pray that I may die a good death, so that I can keep your company [dear husband] and see God in heaven".

Such are some lineaments of the portrait of the romantic world of the Mando - a world of a sophistication and elegance, at once Latin and Indian, that has disappeared and will never return; a world that is barely reminisced by the old and barely comprehensible to the young; a world, with its joys and sorrows, which endured for over a century in Goa's green and pleasant land.

ACKNOWLEDGMENTS

We wish to express our thanks to our sponsors, and to Maria Aurora Couto, Alban Couto, and Uday Bhembro, whose generous help made the publication of this book possible.

ANTHOLOGY: MANDOS OF UNION (*EKVOTT*) AND LAMENTATION (*VILLAP*)

Index, Score, Text and Translation

INDEX OF MANDOS

1. *Mandos of Union* (Ekvott)

2. *Mandos of Lamentation* (Villap)

Ekvott 1

DOMINGOS MASCARENHAS
(1864-1919)

Sarkeanum kituli tum nitolli

1. Sarkeanum kituli tum nitolli
   Korneanim kituli bori
   Ai, doti torhi anim dennem unnem
   Konnem re kelem ulounnem

      Utrachi mudi ajustar keli
      Poili mezun getolom doti
      Anim tuje main-tichi aikolear budi
      Maka motti marta re jintti

2. Cazrachi poili chitti podllea mhunnon
Moje maincho geleo re jintti
Anim anvem mudi tuka dilea Florentin
Ugrhas dor re got-tti

Moje mainum kitem muntllearu
Tum vaitt voronaka
Tuka anim mum re maka khoxi zali
Ternam tonddu zalem re tika

1. How clear in countenance you are, and how good in your deeds! Oh, the dowry is small, and the presents not enough. Now who was it that arranged the match?

I have put the engagement ring on you. I will count the dowry first. When I hear your mother's advice, I have a fit.

2. When the first banns were read, my mother's swoons vanished. Remember well, Florentina, that I have given you the ring.

Whatever rude things my mother may say, you must not mind them. You and I have decided to marry, and that has silenced her.

Commentary, p. 129.

Ekvott 2

MESTRE *JANTU*

Inocenti mujem vido

1. Inocenti mujem vido
Sacrificar kortam tuka
Mujem kalliz re ugot-ttam
Poilem entrad tuka ditam

2. Papan mamanum vinchilo
Maka Devanum nirmilo
Aj amy'm sacramentu zol-llo
Ekvott sagrad amtso zalo

3. Aji disu sontosatso
Sorgary uzvarh noketrantso
Ulas galtam y aum mogatso
Beiju ditam sontosatso

Sol do, sol do, mi re mi
Mogan bounya y amim

1. For you I sacrifice my innocent life. I open my heart and give you the first entry.

2. My father and mother chose you; God destined you for me. We have received the sacrament today. Our union has been made holy.

3. Today is a day of happiness. In heaven there is the light of the stars. I breathe a sigh of love, and give you a kiss of joy.

Sol do, sol do, mi re mi. Let us live in love, you and me.

Commentary, p. 130.

Ekvott 3

AZAVEDO DINIZ
(1860-1907)

Tisri kunvori mum go tum

1. Tisri kunvori mum go tum
   Paigery maingery ekloch morgad y aum-um
   Te tuja gunnam' lagunum
   Disprezar sogleam' kortam mum go y aum-um

2. Sogleanko sanddunum
   Moga tuka getam go gopantum
   Eku anju munnum
   Adorar tuka kortam mum go y aum-um

3. Ful-lleanlem utoro
   Mannyka y anvem kelem go cumpriro
   Suko anim sontos mellunko
   Argam y amim diuya go Devako

Maka mogu tuzo
Muja kallyza' petlla uzo

1. You are the third daughter ["princess"]; I am the only heir of my parents. Because of your lovely gifts, I despise all the others, adored one!

2. Relinquishing all the others, I take you to my bosom, my love. I adore you as I do an angel.

3. I have honored the words of my elders, my jewel. Let us give thanks to God so that we may find happiness and joy.

I love you. My heart is on fire!

Commentary, p. 130.

Ekvott 4

ROQUE CORREIA-AFONSO
(1859-1937)

Bara-tera vorsam zalim

1. Bara-tera vorsam zalim
   Bara diso mum re disle
   Aundde vit-tte kal-lle
   Martirio re bogile
   Devan tsurtsury' amche kele

2. Sagrad utor moga tujem
Ontoskornan samballilem
Vadorho-morho ailem
Vignom legun ailem
Abalaro nuim re zalem

3. Tuja utrary re patielim
Borvonxanum mum re raulim
Tum boro re dekunum
Gopant tuja paulim
Aji feliz mum re zalim

Are yo, yo, yo, yo re moga
Utriketam tuka

1. Many years have passed, twelve and thirteen, though they seemed only twelve days. We yearned and pined, and lived in anguish, and now God has had mercy on us.

2. I gave you my solemn word, and I treasured it in my heart. Storms and tempests came, and affliction too, but we were not shaken.

3. I put my trust in your words and waited in hope. Because you are good, I came to your bosom, and am happy today.

Come, oh come to me, love. I yearn for you.

Commentary, p. 131.

Ekvott 5

ARNALDO DE MENEZES
(1863-1917)

Soglem vido mum re mujem

1. Soglem vido mum re mujem
   Tuja pasun samballilem
   Dolleany'm sangyloly'm utor amchem
   Sodanch monantum dovorchem

2. Tuka tsoile tedech vella
Sonsar zai-i zalo maka
Muji birmoti genaka
Cazrach'm utor ditam tuka

3. Morhgonvantum muzo gaum-um
Simpatizar zalom y aum-um
Doti tokrhi zaleary zaum-um
Tuj' lagy'm cazar zatol'm y aum-um

4. Ugrhas keleary mum re mannyka
Daduskai bogta muja jiva'
Maka fatti tum korynaka
Dusreach' nattkai aikum naka

Forench utor dileary maka
At-paim' zoroin feliz kortol'm tuka

1. I saved my whole life for you. The word we spoke with our eyes - let us always keep in our minds.

2. The moment I saw you, I began to love life (lit. I wanted the world). Do not reject me and suffer the curse of my unhappiness. I give you my promise to marry you.

3. Morhgoum/Margão is your town. I felt affection for you. Even though the dowry be small, I will marry you.

4. When I think of you, my jewel, joy fills my life. Do not turn away from me. Do not listen to people's spiteful talk.

If you will give me your word, I will wear out my hands and feet to make you happy.

Commentary p. 131.

Ekvott 6

GIZELINO REBELO
(1875-1931)

Diso ekleponnantule

1. Diso ekleponnantule
Aji san cabar maka zale
E ulas kallyzache
Sodankal Devan sompadile

2. Sacramentach' ekvottanum
Dogaim y aji borlim re kurpenum
Devachery patieunum
Furhasunchem borve korum' gunnom

3. Papa morun muzo gelo
Retrat punn dekil'nam mamantso
Adar magotam tuzo
Aum-um-im ditol'm tuka muzo

Sorginch'm besaum
Amchery porhchem
Sodanch y amim dadusponnan bounchem

1. The days of my single life have come to an end today. God has forever ended our hearts' sighs!

2. In the union of the sacrament, we have both been filled with grace. With our trust in God, let us go forward to do well.

3. My father is dead, and I have not seen even a picture of my mother. I ask for your support, and I too will give you mine.

May heaven's blessing descend upon us, and may we always live in joy.

Commentary, p. 132.

Ekvott 7

GIZELINO REBELO
(1875-1931)

Lanom burgeponnam sanum

1. Lanom burgeponnam sanum
Diso y anvem kal-lle feliz zaunum
At'm y aum galtam porgottunum
Mujem kalliz curasaum-om

2. Pitamm kal-llol' mak' sorgari
   Atam kitea' urhoil' re margari
   Borvons' dovon-n Devacheri
   Ulas galtam noketranri

3. Papa morun muzo gelo
   Maman maka cazar mum re kelo
   Mogats' sangat sodun dilo
   Devan sasvot keleary puro

   Magnnem y aum-um koritam Devako
   Suseg y amkam mellcha' furharako

1. From my early years as a child, I passed my days in happiness. I now declare in public what is in my heart.

2. In the past you had taken me up into heaven: why have you now cast me by the wayside? Placing my trust in God, I breathe a sigh at my stars!

3. My father is dead, and my uncle married me. I have sought love's company - may God make it everlasting.

I pray God that we may find peace in the future.

Commentary, p. 132.

Ekvott 8

GIZELINO REBELO
(1875-1931)

Nirmit zaunum re Devachem

1. Nirmit zaunum re Devachem
   Gorhit zaly'm amcha cazrachem
   Te tuja moganum y attapolam
   Soglench ontoskornom mujem

2. O ekvott re sukatso
Anjam' porim samballuntso
Sacrament aj amim unir kelo
Utrikeanim nirmilolo

3. Noketranim surngailolea
Muja furharacha y anja
Ankvarponn sanddun sodil' tuka
Aji sontosacha disa

Vido y amchem
Eklech Devako bettoichem

1. God ordaining it, our marriage was arranged. My whole inner being has been wrapt up in your love.

2. We must protect our joyous union like angels. We have today united our sacrament, created by our yearning.

3. Angel of my future life, adorned with stars! I have surrendered my maiden life and sought you out on this happy day.

Our life - let us offer it to God alone.

Commentary, p. 133.

Ekvott 9

GIZELINO REBELO
(1875-1931)

Sontos bogta re jivako

1. Sontos bogta re jivako
   Uzvarh petlla e gorako
   Daduskaienum bounchako
   Magnnem y amim korya re Devako

2. Ankvarponnom bolanddunum
   Tsolya kurpecha marganum
   Estolacha re pontanum
   Ekttaim amchem zalem curasaum-om

3. Sacramentu ekvottatso
Zaleary puro uzvarhatso
Sangat korun ekmekatso
Sodanch feliz karhya diso

Pormoll jazmintso
Mogureantso
Sodanch Devan samballuntso

1. Joy surges in my heart, and our house glows with light. Let us pray to God to always live in happiness.

2. Changing our single life, let us walk on the path of grace. The tip of the stole has joined our hearts today.

3. May the sacrament of union be one of light. In each other's company, let us happily pass our days!

The perfume of jasmines and Arabian jasmines,
may God ever preserve it!

Commentary, p. 133.

Ekvott 10

GIZELINO REBELO
(1875-1931)

Surya sontosan udelo

1. Surya sontosan udelo
   Noketranim cercar taka kelo
   Santanch' bogtanch' uzvarhanum
   Amim sacramentu gexlo

2. Ankvarponnom sompadilem
Dogainch'm amchem kalliz unir zalem
Em gorhit furharachem
Amkam Devan nirmilolem

3. Amtso ekvott re zauchako
Painom-mainom zaite gexle koxtto
Mirhmirhy' bogtai muj' kallyzako
Baunddants' sangat sandduchako

Sukanum bounchem
Moganum rauchem
Eksurponn chintun y amchem

1. The sun rose joyfully and the stars encircled it. In the light of the saints and the blessed we received the holy sacrament.

2. Our single life has ended. Our two hearts have become one. God destined this future event for us.

3. Our parents worked much to make our union come true. It hurts my heart to leave the company of my brothers and sisters.

Let us walk in joy and live in love, thinking of how lonely we are.

Commentary, p. 134.

Ekvott 11

GIZELINO REBELO
(1875-1931)

Suryan uzvarhu dampilo

1. Suryan uzvarhu dampilo
   Noketrantso porzoll fankarolo
   Maiach' pantsve torkery disa
   Tumim sacramentu zol-llo

2. Sodanch estad re cazratso
Sacrament bangran surngailolo
Devach' mogan rochilolo
Aj to tumkam favo zalo

3. Sodanch pormollu mogreantso
Gumgumm zoborh yeta re tsampeantso
Aji disu sontosatso
Prosperaro tumkam zautso

4. Aji sontosacha disa
Felicitar korum' aileam tuka
Tum cazar zal' munn moga
Tuja amigam' visrum' naka

O porzoll sorgintso
Devan tumkam conservar kortso

1. The sun has hidden its light; the stars flash their brilliance. On the fifth day of May, the two of you received the sacrament.

2. The married state is always a sacrament adorned with gold. Created by God's love, it was destined for you today.

3. There is ever the perfume of Arabian jasmines and a strong aroma of champaks. May this day of bliss ever prosper for you.

4. I have come on this happy day to wish you well. Because you are now married, dear boy, do not forget your brethren.

The brightness of heaven - made God preserve it for us!

Commentary, p. 135.

Ekvott 12

TORQUATO DE FIGUEIREDO
(1876-1948)

Derfente uzvarh fankarolo

1. Derfente uzvarh fankarolo
   Gopam' surya muj' udelo
   Cazrats' sacramentu zol-llo
   Tuka muzo poti kornum gexlo

2. Inocenti vido mujem
Moga bettoich'm tuka pol-llem
Em gorhit moga y amchem
Sorgary furhem talhar re zalolem

3. Lotllech' bairi y aum-um sorlim
Bitory sorlim Kurhtoreantum
Sogleam' dispidiro kornum
Ailim moga tuja re gopantum

Zaleary puro ekvott y amtso
Devach' besanvantso

1. All of a sudden a light shone, and the sun rose in my bosom. We received the marriage sacrament and I made you my husband.

2. I have had to devote to you my pure life, love; for this our destiny was beforehand shaped for us in heaven.

3. I leave Lotlli/Loutulim and enter Kurhtori/Curtorim. Taking leave of all, I rush into your arms.

May our union be one of God's blessing.

Commentary, p. 135.

Ekvott 13

TORQUATO DE FIGUEIREDO
(1876-1948)

Sontos bogta re jivako

1. Sontos bogta re jivako
Ekvott y aji zala munnum y amtso
Zaleary puro besanvantso
Amtso sacrament cazratso

2. Amchi soiriko korunko
Zaite moga gexle tunvem koxtto
Follu yeunum tuj' koxttantso
Paulim tuja re sangtako

3. Soireanch' bitory mak' vinchili
Potinny mum re zaucha' tum mogachi
Sangtach' zali moga foxi
Gorkany zaucha' ya gorachi

Feliz y amim karhcha' diso
Ugrhas korya re Devatso

1. Happiness surges in my life because our union has come to pass today. May our sacrament of marriage become one of blessing.

2. You took great pains to bring about our betrothal, my love. Your efforts bore fruit, and I now come to join you.

3. They chose me from among our kinsfolk to be your loving wife. I yearned for your company, my love, and to be mistress in this house.

To spend our days in happiness, let us remember God.

Commentary, p. 135.

Ekvott 14

TORQUATO DE FIGUEIREDO
(1876-1948)

Suryan uzvarh fankarolo

1. Suryan uzvarh fankarolo
   Noketrantso porzoll purean pol-llo
   Cazrats' sacramentu gexlo
   Amtso ekvott mum re zalo

2. Nimann' visvas tuj' tivatso
Aji y amim sontosanum pal-llo
Furhench Devan taka velo
Anim kotta muje mainko!

3. Aum mogu kortam tuzo
Tosoch mogu tunvuim kory re muzo
Mogu kornum ekmekatso
Cazrats' sacrament samballtso

Anjanch' porim ekvott y amtso
Zaleary puro sodanch besanvantso

1. The light has blazed with the sun, and the splendor of the stars has dimmed. We have received the marriage sacrament and our union has been achieved.

2. Today we have honored your uncle's last wish. God took him away too soon, and alas, my mother!

3. I love you, and do you also love me. Loving each other we will protect our marriage sacrament.

Our union is as one of angels. May it ever be one of blessing!

Commentary, p. 136.

Ekvott 15

PASCOAL NORONHA
(1872-1936)

Paicha maincha moreantulim

1. Paicha maincha moreantulim
   Aichan bairi y aum-um sorlim
   Em chintunum dukam golloilim
   Itlean tangely' soireanch' conta' pol-llim

2. Tsolyant poilem y aum-um follo
   Paich'-mainch' y asa maka bollo
   Kitlench nibor marleary re morho
   Dakoichako sonsum' nuim munn zorho

3. Sonsrantulo distin y amtso
   Foxalponnan cumprir kortso
   Amcha patkan aileary re uzo
   Dusreats' kedim' guneaum nuim re kortso

4. Kitlich dekichi zaleari
   Tsukun samporhye utrari
   Mujem kitench vaxtto disleari
   Cabar korchem amizadi bitori

1. I have come out today from father's and mother's sheltering care. The thought of this brought tears to my eyes. From today I shall be one of my husband's family.

2. Among the daughters the first fruit, I have my parents' strength in me. However violent the storm, we must show that it is not hard to withstand.

3. Let us cheerfully fulfill our life's destiny. If fire rises through our own fault, let us never blame others for it.

4. However well brought up, we can, erring, say the wrong word. Whatever you find bad in me, let us resolve it in friendship.

Commentary, p. 136.

Ekvott 16

PASCOAL NORONHA
(1872-1936)

Amcha gorchanche foxenum

1. Amcha gorchanche foxenum
   Ekvott y amtso kelo Igorjenum
   Vorhanch'm magnnem aikily'm Devanum
   Diunum tankam chintyloly'm foxalponnom

2. Atam kaido mum re y amtso
   Desej tantso corresponder kortso
   Bangrach' daiek adar unttitso
   Axleary puro adaru kurpetso

3. Sogleam noureanko sanddunum
Painum muja kal-ll' tuka vintsunum
Boukon-n tuja gunnanko tsoinum
Tum maka feliz kortol' munnum

4. Novim nim amy'm ekmukako
Follam koxim zaloly'm ek rukako
Ked'nnom tsuki zaleary utrako
Defeit diutsnim bailea sonsarako

1. Our family wishing it, the Church has joined us together. God has heard our elders' prayers, giving them the happiness they desired.

2. Our duty now is to carry out their wishes. Even a pestle of gold needs the support of a mortar wall. May we always have the help of grace!

3. Rejecting all suitors, my father chose you, having in mind your fine personal gifts, and knowing that you will make me happy.

4. We are not strangers to each other, but rather like fruits growing on the same tree. If I should ever say the wrong word [say something offensive] we must not let the outside world know.

Commentary, p. 137.

Ekvott 17

JOAQUIM SANTANA MENEZES
(1898-1939)

Sodanch chintitalim y aum-um

1. Sodanch chintitalim y aum-um
   Ganvam' istruido tsoli munnum
   Em muj'm Devan grandezo tsounum
   Galy' mak' unneponnantum

      Papa-mamam' foxi dekunum
      Tanche utor morhinam re y aum-um

2. Sodanch naxloly' maka foxi
Castam' bairi cazar re zaupachi
Papan-maman atacar keli
Meltt' munn durhuvanchi raxi

Atam oso aila sonsaru
Axleary puro instrusaum y anim durhu

3. Atam somjily'm re chitunum
Advam' ekloch rochlol' munn Devanum
Kely'naim sudir tsad-ddi bambonnom
Soglich sonsrach' fottvonnom

Castam y amim galya re poro
Mogach' suka' vegim maka voro

1. I had always thought that I was the only educated girl in the village. Seeing this proud position of mine, God brought me to humiliation.

As my parents wish it, I will not cross their wishes.

2. I was always set against marrying outside caste. Father and mother insisted, because, they said, I get heaps of money.

This is what the world has come to! All that people want is education and cash.

3. I have understood now that God created Adam alone. No Shudras did He make, or Tsad-ddi/Chardos or Brahmins - all this is the world's falsehood!

Let us put caste aside. Take me at once to the pleasures of love!

Commentary, p. 137.

Ekvott 18

FRANCISCO SARDINHA
(1897-1958)

Aji pasun Devachery patieunum

1. Aji pasun Devachery patieunum
Sonxitaly'm mujem burgeponnom
Sorgim surya-noketram' tsounum
Vellu muzo passar kortaly'm y aum-um

Vadorho-morho aileary re moga
Kedninch y aum sandduch'm nam re tuka

1. Trusting in God, I have till now borne my youth with patience. I passed the time of the day looking at the sun and stars in the sky.

Though storms assail us, love, I will never abandon you.

Commentary, p. 138.

Villap 1

LUÍS MENEZES
(1866-1936)

Sonsar charich re disantso

1. Sonsar charich re disantso
   Ugrhas vosnam motintulo
   Tunvem keloleam korneantso Marianinh
   Koxtto-dogdantso

2. Segredanum kelo tratu
   Modem papan gexlo gatu
   Kallyza' bale marnum satu Marianinh
   Sanddil' sangatu

3. Anjach' porim kelo mogu
   Utrikeanim gexlo beiju
   Pixa' porim kitea' bounta Marianinh
   Tunttoun kallizu

4. Maka vollvollailo Saiba
   Kurhi atmeam soitu
   Anim itule koxtt bogle Marianinh
   Gorje viretu

5. Adeus adeus muja moga
Dispidir kortam tuka
Te koxtt bogtai te maka Marianinh
Dogd bogum' tuka

1. The span of life is so brief [lit. the world is of four days only]! The misery and pain that you caused me, do not leave me, Marianinha!

2. We planned to marry, in secret, when your father butted in and stopped it [lit. father, in the middle, betrayed us]. Seven swords pierced my heart, Marianinha, and we parted.

3. I loved you as an angel. I kissed you with yearning. How can you go like one demented, Marianinha, rending my heart like this!

4 I have been tormented, Lord, both in body and soul. All these sorrows, Marianinha, I bore to no purpose at all.

5. Good-bye, good-bye, my love. I take leave of you. May the heartaches you made me feel become yours too!

Commentary, p. 139.

Villap 2

ANAMU/ANONYMOUS

Maingeri paigeri

1. Maingeri paigeri
   Tsoleant y eklich y aum-um tsoli
   Ai, muji osoli tsoli mellum' tsolea'
   Bagi kituly' zai-i!

2. Doti munttai torhi
   Tsoli sarkean kituly' bori
   Ai, irmancha punnum adranum maka
   Cazar koreai-i

3. Maim-im y anim pai-i
   Dogaim dukan golloitai-i
   Ai, kosolem Deva disgrazo mujem
   Amiganim mak' sandduchem

1. I am the only girl among the boys born to my parents. Ah, to get a girl like me - how much luck does a boy not need!

2. "The dowry is not much," they say. "The girl is so beautiful to look at". Oh, get me married, please, with my elder brother's help.

3. Mother and father are both silently weeping. My God, what misery is this, for my friends have deserted me!

Commentary, p. 139.

Villap 3

ANAMU/ANONYMOUS

Zaite sukanum varholim

1. Zaite sukanum varholim
   Titlinch y aum disgrasado zalim
   Im dukam ge rogtachim
   Tim mamam tuka ge lagtolim

2. Janot dixtti porhtrich moga
   E muja orhdeant fugar zata
   Mamam kitem tum chintita
   Papa muzo rorhum' boisol' saiba

3. Utriketaly'm aum cazrako
Mamam muji zainam re cedero ...

> Nam, nam, nam, nam nam
> Cazar kori nam
> Tuje oslench infern e sonsram' nam

TSOLI: 1. I grew up in great happiness, but since have fallen into disgrace. These tears of blood, mother, will stick to you.

2. When I see you well dressed, love, I feel choked in my breast. What are you thinking, mother. Father has sat down to cry!

3. I yearned for marriage, but mother will not yield....

MOTHER: No, no, no and no! I will never marry you. There is no hell on earth like you!

Commentary, p. 140.

Villap 4

PAULO MILAGRES SILVA
(1855-1931)

Tsondrimm kupam' fankarolo

1. Tsondrimm kupam' fankarolo
   Vellatso uzvarhu dankolo
   E tuj' mogako lagunum
   Muzo distin perder kelo

2. Mujem vido cabar kelem
   Te tuja moga' re pasunum
   Nimanny'm utor tuka dilem
   Tuj' bogor konnonch nam re munnum

3. Anjach'm sarkem tujem tsounum
Pixa porim bountam mum re y aum-um
Tuje lagim cazar zaunum
Suko bogit'm y axlol'm y aum-um

Maim-im muntta mogach' maka
Nak' fobor
Sonsar zalo re cabaro

1. The moon shone in the clouds, and the light of the sun was hidden. For love of you, I ruined my destiny.

2. For love of you I wore down my life. I gave you my last word, that there is no one for me but you.

3. Seeing your angel face, I go around like a madman. In marrying you I could have experienced happiness.

Mother says, no talk of love for me, and so my life's joy ends.

Commentary, p. 140.

Villap 5

ANAMU/ANONYMOUS

Ek dis bagint y aum gelolim

1. Ek dis bagint y aum gelolim
Torhim getlim anvem abolim
Tinvim aum geun yetalim
Eka tsolean magun velim

2. Abolim ditannam aum rol-llim
Maka zai munn anvem al-llelim
Donim utram motintum gol-llim
Tednam ankvar aum asul-lim

3. Ernest tuje lagim aum magtam
Moji kakutt kor munn atam
Cazrachê adim direit magtam
Dukanim dukanim aum rorhtam

Falea aum abolim arhtolim
Tuka ditolim
Tumger gara konnum asai re
Fulam malttolim

1. I went one day to the garden and plucked a few *abolem* flowers. I was coming home with them, when a young gentleman asked for and took them.

2. I wept while I gave him the flowers, because I had brought them for myself. Two words formed in my mind, for I was unmarried then.

3. Ernesto, I pray you, take pity on me. I ask for this right before your marriage, and I cry with tears welling from my eyes, oh, such tears!

I will bring the flowers tomorrow and give them to you. Who have you at home who wears flowers?

Commentary, p. 141.

Villap 6

CÉSAR-MENDES

Dony-tinim muinnem zale muj' moga

1. Dony-tinim muinnem zale muj' moga
   Fobor naxleary maka
   Eky punn chitti darhy re maka
   Mogach'm utor diunum mannyka
   Nam zaleary jivu ditam tuka

2. Zoborhi maka asa re foxi
   Morhgovantum rauchi
   Papak y asa mum re foxi
   Seminarintum maka galchi
   Ai, ai, y ai, moti zata pixi

3. Dony'm tinim chitteo dal-lleo muj' moga
César Pinhakorhe
Respost pauly'm nam muje korhe
Dukany'm bortai muje dolle
Responder korchi zaleary polle

4. Xi, xi, xi, xi, xi Césaru Pinho
Kitem tunvem kelem
Denunciaro kelem konnem
Dolleank yeta muja ron-nnem
Mary'-Elen [Maria Helena] fapaily'm tuka konnem

5. Sato maldisaum' galtam muj' moga
Denunciar kel' taka
Koslem dizgras muja Deva
Fonddach' degery pautam dista
Suicidar zauchem maka dista

6. Yo, yo, yo, yo, muj' moga
Abras di re maka
Juramentu ditam tuka
Kednonch sanddtso nam munn moga
Mary'-Elen kallzach' muja gondda

7. Intrujice aum-um korum' lagotam
Mamako fottoitam
Pneumoni zalea munn sangotam
Rogtam vonkunum dakoitam
Seminarint vosnam munn sangotam

8. Raty cabar zaunum dis y ail' muj' moga
Nido pon-nnam maka
Muzo papa marum' yeta
Dispidiro kortam tuka
Adeus, adeus, adeus muja moga

1. My love, it is nearly three months now that I have not heard from you. Write me at least one letter, and give me one loving word, else I will kill myself for your sake!

2. I have a great wish to live in Morhgoum. But father is set in putting me into the Seminary. Oh, oh, my mind is nearly going mad!

3. My darling, I sent you two or three letters with César Pinho. No reply reached me. My eyes brim with tears. See if you can write me an answer.

4. Shame, shame on you, César Pinho! What have you done? Was it you who betrayed me? Tears come to my eyes. Who was it that beat you, Maria Helena?

5. I call down seven curses on the man who betrayed me! What wretchedness is this, my God! I feel I am on the brink of the tomb. I feel an urge to suicide!

6. Come, come to me my love, and embrace me. I swear to you that I will never leave you, Maria Helena, my heart's bud!

7. For your sake, I will plot and scheme. I will lie to my mother. I will tell them that I have pneumonia, and force myself to vomit blood. I will refuse to go to the Seminary.

8. Night has ended, adored one, and the day dawns. I can get no sleep. My father comes to beat me. I now bid you farewell. Good-bye, good-bye, my love!

Commentary, p. 142.

Villap 7

ARNALDO DE MENEZES
(1863-1917)

Ai, kitem y anvem korchem

1. Ai, kitem y anvem korchem?
   Fuim vosun y anvem morchem?
   Kedy'm vol-lly'm dizgras mum re mujem
   Atam konnanko sanguchem?

2. Mateach'm fulam mujim baulim
   Atach'm kanknnam mujim funtllim
   Tondda' utram cabar zalim
   Dolleanch'm dukam dekun suklim

3. Ai, kitem y anvem kelem?
   Ai, kitem Deva zalem?
   Unneponnom itulem
   Atam bogitam guneaum vinnem

   Nagoili Saiba
   Sogli giraxili maka

1. Lord, what shall I do? Where shall I go and die? And this disaster of mine - who shall I tell it to?

2. The flowers on my head have wilted. The bangles on my hand have been smashed. The words have faded from my lips, and even the tears have dried in my eyes.

3. Oh, what have I done? My God, what happened? Such depths of abjectness do I now suffer without fault.

I have been cheated, Lord; I have been wholly betrayed!

Commentary, p. 143.

Villap 8

ARNALDO DE MENEZES
(1863-1917)

The Adolfinian Trilogy, 1
Tuzo mogu axlol' munnum

1. Tuzo mogu axlol' munnum
Morhgounts' borla sogloch gaum-um
Kallyzach' gutto tuje mujery dovornum
Y atam morum' paulam y aum-um

    Ai, ai, ontoskornanche gave re muje
    Ai, y ai, konnanko dakoiche

2. Moti zaucha' paulea pixi
Tunvem dusreach' kely' munn y axi
Tuje mainko zoborhy zoborhy zaly' foxi
Enddeach' ruka' fursary marchi

    Ai, ai, kallyzache atam sintmento muje
    Ai, y ai, konnanko sanguche

3. Paich'-mainch' moti zalea tontti
Dekun korum' pauli fatti
Camilachi tannim y aikun fotti
Maka eucha' paulea valtti

    Ai, ai, kurhiche y atam vollvolle muje
    Ai, y ai, Devan curar korche

4. Adeus korum' nuzo tuka
Kitea' sanddun vot' re maka
Mujem vido y anvem bettoiloly'm tuka
Adelin muja mannyka!

    Ai, ai, dukache y atam vallo re muje
    Ai, y ai, Devanum somzuche

1. Morhgoum/Margão is full of the news that I loved you. I have carried the secrets of your heart on myself, and from this have been brought near to my death.

Oh, the wounds in my heart! Oh, to whom shall I show them?

2. My mind has nearly gone mad because you loved another. Your mother wanted so much to crucify you to the *Erondd* tree!

Oh, the aches in my soul! Oh, to whom shall I confide them?

3. Your father and mother are out of their minds: that is why they have set themselves against me. They listened to Camilo's lies and this has ruined me (lit. termites have come to me).

Oh, the torments of my body! Oh, may God relieve me of them!

4. I cannot say farewell to you. Oh why are you deserting me? My life was consecrated to you, Adelina, my love!

Oh, the floods of my tears - oh, only God can understand them!

Commentary, p. 144.

Villap 9

ARNALDO DE MENEZES
(1863-1917)

The Adolfinian Trilogy, 2
Motim'-sopnnantum naxlolem

1. Motim'-sopnnantum naxlolem
Ondum Devan dizgras mujery dal-llem
Em muj'm bangaro untsa molachem
Sompeponnim korhun gelem

    Sonsrach' y aso sanddily' re puta
    Sorgary eky punn zapo di re maka

2. Sangun cabar korum' nuzo
E muje kallyzache dogdogo
Umalleari eunum umallo
Deva zalem dizolvero

    Sonsrach' y aso sanddily' re moga
    Sorgary eky punn zapo di re maka

3. Muji birmoty funttum' tuka
Trair tunvem kelol' dekun maka
Recebimentacha tuja vella
Muje sirap bett'tlei tuka

    Sonsrach' y aso sanddily' re puta
    Sorgary eky punn zapo di re maka

4. Kalliz bettoilolea y anja
Dispidir kortam y aum-um tuka
Ganttech' far zatai tedech vella
Mujem vido melnnam tuka

    Itlean sonsar sompol' re puta
    Adeus y adeus y Adelin muja y anja

1. Undreamt of and unexpectedly, God this year sent misfortune on me. This priceless gold of mine simply melted and flowed away.

    I have lost all joy in life, my dear one. In heaven, at least, say a word to me.

2. I cannot come to an end in speaking of the agony in my heart. Seething blasts of heat, one upon another, have melted it, my God!

> I have lost all joy in life, my dear one. In heaven, at least, say a word to me.

3. The curse of my misfortune will burden you, because you have betrayed me. At the time of your wedding, my curses will cleave to you.

> I have lost all joy in life, my dear one. In heaven, at least, say a word to me.

4. Angel of my heart's devotion, I now bid you farewell. When the wedding bells ring, you will have lost me forever.

> With this, the world ends for me, my beloved. Farewell, Adelina my love.

Commentary, p. 147.

Villap 10

ARNALDO DE MENEZES
(1863-1917)

The Adolfinian Trilogy, 3
Chintun furhar Deva muzo

1. Chintun furhar Deva muzo
   Rorhtam muja zalolea disako
   Bou kon-n vellach' muja gunnan-
   Ko y anim nixttur noketranko

2. Rorhun dukanch' kortam vallo
Susegu nam muja jivako
Fatti kely' anvem sonsrako
Pavoi y anjam'-borhveam' sangatako

3. Vollvolly' mirhmirhe jivache
Atam Deva konnanko sanguche
Avivaro zatai gave
E muja gagur kallizache

4. E muj' dukancha tempari
Vellanum keli re molbotti
Infelizo dekun sorti
Y atam Deva kakultty muji kori

Sonsranum sanddilo maka
Mujem vid mellonam re tuka

1. Thinking of my future, I mourn for the day I was born; above all, for the portent of that moment and for the malignant stars.

2. Streams of tears well from my weeping. My life knows no peace. I have turned my back upon the world, so take me now to the company of the angels.

3. The agonies and heartbreaks of life - to whom, Lord, shall I tell about them? My sensitive heart's wounds become raw again.

4. At this time of my sorrow, the sun has been darkened. My destiny being an unhappy one, take pity on me now, Lord.

The world has forsaken me. My life will never be yours (lit. you will never get my life).

Commentary, p. 148.

Villap 11

ARNALDO DE MENEZES
(1863-1917)

Sintment varoily' e sonsrako

1. Sintment varoily' e sonsrako
Tsounuz' duk y ek tuj' dolleanko
Gagur dekun kalllizo
Dogdog e muj' bogtai-i kurhiko

2. Dukestanchem vido y amchem
Ek punn suk nam mak' kurhichem
Sonsrant piraxito korchem
Sorgary amim ekttaim mum re zauchem

3. Tsoilea' bogor e sonsrantum
Eku dis bolanddum' nuzo
Kedonn' vellu melloto
Gopant e muj' ulaso galchako

4. Sanddun vosum' mujan nuzo
Mogu bedla muj' kallyzako
Ugrhas maka yeta tuzo
Raty-dis rorhun cabar kel' jiu muzo

Ugrhas mujan visrum' nuzo
Beijanim ximpylolea kallyzatso

1. I poured out my feelings on the world, and cannot bear to see a tear in your eyes. As my heart is sensitive, torments afflict my poor body.

2. Our life is of the unhappy ones, and not one earthly joy have we. Let us do penance in this world, and be united in heaven.

3. Unless I see you in this world, I cannot live through a single day. When will I find the time to breathe these sighs into your bosom?

4. I cannot leave you, because love has embedded itself in my heart. The memory of you comes to me. I have worn out my life weeping through nights and days.

I cannot forget the memory of you, and of your heart, watered by my kisses!

Commentary, p. 149.

Villap 12

ARNALDO DE MENEZES
(1863-1917)

Soglem vido mujem tsounum

1. Soglem vido mujem tsounum
   Rorhtam odruxtto chintunum
   Boguch'm y axlolem bogunum
   Raut'm y aum Devachery patieunum

2. Sonsrach' volloky aili maka
   Sonsar naka mum re maka
   Devan kitea' dovorl' maka
   Osoly' dukach' muja tempa'

3. Kosli buzvonnom nam maka
Tsurtsureancha muja kallyza
Kitem bogum' y anvem Saiba
E muj' burgeponnanch' tempa'

4. Joban bogyloly'm te baxenum
Atam bogum' paulom y aum-um
Adeus y adeus sogttam' kornum
Sorginch' paundde mejtam y aum-um

Soglem Deva bettoitam tuka
Sanddynak' maka

1. Looking back on my life I weep, brooding over my misfortune. I have suffered what was in store for me, and now I await the mercy of God.

2. I know now what life means, and I love it no more. Why has God kept me alive at such a time of my affliction?

3. I have no consolation. Oh, my poor heart! What have I to suffer, Lord, at the time of my youth?

4. As Job suffered, so do I suffer now. Taking leave of all, I count the rungs of the ladder to heaven.

I offer everything to you, Lord. Do not abandon me.

Commentary, p. 149.

Villap 13

ARNALDO DE MENEZES
(1863-1917)

Oromb nuim re y amcha Gointso

1. Oromb nuim re y amcha Gointso
   Dusrea' feliz mum re tsoutso
   O xirap nuim konnantso
   Gunnum y amcha zalolea terratso

   Sonsrach' funnom kol-lli re maka
   Suko naka

2. Ya disgrasach' tempantum
Devan rochlol' mak' sonsrantum
Nixturaietso vellu polleunum
Guttu sangtam y aum rorhunum

Bexttech fobro kelolei tunvem
Te tempantum

3. Doriant laranche gorhgorho
Kalliz zalam utsambollo
Osoly' birankullaiecha vellari
Konnom nam muja y adrako

Boguch'm y axloly'm boglem tuka
Tsoi-nak' maka

4. Konixttaienum jieuchem
Sorginch'm dero y amy'm tankuchem
Santanch'm vido y amy'm chintuchem
Vegysar y amim moronnom maguchem

Patkanch'm bogosonny'm magun re amim
Sorgary tsouchem

1. It is not natural for our Goa to suffer another's welfare. This is not anyone's curse, but a quality native to the land of our birth.

I have discovered what the world stands for (lit. I have known the world's sign). I reject the world!

2. At this time of sorrow, God gave me life on this earth. Seeing the time of malediction, I tell my story with tears.

You told false tales at that time.

3. There is a thunder of waves in the sea. My heart becomes restless. There is none to help me at this fearful moment in my life.

You have got what you deserved. Do not look at me!

4. We must live in distress, and reach the gate of heaven. We must reflect on the lives of the saints and pray for an early death.

Asking pardon for our sins, we must look towards heaven.

Commentary, p. 149.

Villap 14

GIZELINO REBELO
(1875-1931)

Koslem vido mum re amchem

1. Koslem vido mum re amchem
   Chintleary moronn fursavelem
   Permissavom Devagelem
   Burgeponnim ulasuchem

2. Itle koxtto bolanddunum
Diso kal-lle fugar zaunum
Em kosoly'm maldisanvom
Xirap lagtai te baxenum

3. Panneam' porim dukam y amchim
Ekleach Devanum somzuchim
Visvasunum y amche modem
Suko zorhya tem sasnachem

Atam Deva sanddunaka
Osolea okantacha vella

1. What a life ours is, a real death on the cross - the decree of God - to be sighed at from childhood!

2. Living through so many agonies, I have passed my days in suffocation. What a malediction is this, that curses seem to cling to me so!

3. Our tears are like water, and only God can know what they mean. Let us then, with hope in our hearts, gain the bliss of heaven.

Abandon me not, oh God, at such a time of my affliction!

Commentary, p. 150.

Villap 15

GIZELINO REBELO
(1875-1931)

Chintun cabar korum' nuzo

1. Chintun cabar korum' nuzo
   Mirhmirhy' bogtai te kallyzako
   Vellu ail' mujery dukantso
   Deva' pasun ugrhas yenam muzo

2. Amizade nam maka dusreachi
   Ekleach muja re jivachi
   Porhdesponnatum jieuchi
   Eklich Deva sorti mum re muji

3. Osolea burgeponnantum
   Suseg nam maka sonsrantum
   Paixaum rigol'm muj' kallyzantum
   Tsoicha' vocha' nimannea garantum

Vollvolle jivache
Atam Deva konnanko sanguche

1. I cannot stop thinking of the pangs that my heart feels! A time of sorrow has come upon me, and even God does not remember me.

2. I have the friendship of no one, only of my own life. To live abandoned - this, my God, is my sole destiny.

3. In such a time, my youth, I have no peace in this world. A passion has got into me - to journey to our final abode.

The pangs of my life! To whom shall I tell them now, my God!

Commentary, p. 150.

Villap 16

GIZELINO REBELO
(1875-1931)

Kakultty tsoiyai tumim muji

1. Kakultty tsoiyai tumim muji
Fasti karhtam dukacha konndachi
Oxi sorti dekun muji
Axa dorynam furharachi

2. Koslem odxruxtt mum re mujem
Sodanch konixttaienum jieuchem
Eksurponnom chintùn mujem
Ron-nnem yet mirhmirheanchem

3. Sonsar kitea' fottoit' re maka
Evei muja burgeponnancha tempa'
Fator-mati rorhtai maka
Noxib pol-llam muj'm paintolla'

Sukach' saulli nam re maka
Soglea muja zolmancha tempa'

1. Look (people) at my affliction, for I go through the troubles of the pool of sorrow [the world]. As this is the fate destined for me, I have no yearning for tomorrow.

2. What a curse mine is, to live in despair always! When I think of my loneliness, I feel like crying in anguish.

3. Why does the world deceive me, even now, the time of my dereliction? Mud and stone weep for me, for my destiny has sunk to my feet.

Not for me even the shadow of joy for the whole length of my life.

Commentary, p. 151.

Villap 17

GIZELINO REBELO
(1875-1931)

Foxalborit bountai y amim

1. Foxalborit bountai y amim
Amkam mel-lleaim soglim dennim
Sontos zala sompeponnim
Magnnim kornum Deva lagim

Tsoiyai loka
Porzolleta
Y amgery uzvarh fankarota

2. I vatto pormollachi
Saulli sorgincha sukachi
Jinsam porinch' kan-nnum fasti
Atam zolttai diamanti

Tsoiyai loka
Porzolleta
Amgery uzvarh fankarota

3. Amcha yetai dolleankorhe
E te mirhmirhe vollvolle
Kituly' dadus bountai polle
Atam' geunum motianch' zole

Tsoiyai loka
Porzolleta
Y amgery uzvarh fankarota

4. Kosoly'm dizgras y amchery ailem
Ekleach Devan nuim re dal-llem
Upau nastonn' boguch'm pol-llem
Osoly'm emkondd garantulem

Tsoiyai loka
Dusman taltta
Amgery inferno vosvota

1. We live in happiness, for we have all good things. Our joy has been found so easily, by just praying to God.

Look, people, it flashes. A light blazes among us!

2. This is the path of perfume, the shadow of heavenly joy. We have lived through much trouble, and now diamonds glitter!

Look, people, it flashes. A light blazes among us!

3. That anguish and those pains appear before our eyes. Look how happy they are, holding jewel clusters in their hands!

Look, people, it flashes. A light blazes among us!

4. What a misfortune has come upon us, God alone could have sent it! We are doomed to suffer, with no choice, this hell in a home.

Look, people, the devil rages. Hell vomits fire among us!

Commentary, p. 151.

Villap 18

TORQUATO DE FIGUEIREDO
(1876-1948)

Soglem mujem vido chintunum

1. Soglem mujem vido chintunum
Dukan bountam y aum-um
Sonsram' maka nam re konnom
Diucha' buzavonnom

2. Sonsar soglo dista re foro
   Dukachem konddo
   Konn punn maka nam sangtolo
   Asa munn felizo

3. Devan maka rochil' tedonnom
   Pol-llom y aum dukantum
   Felecidade mellot kedonnom
   Cabar zatrich y aum-um

4. Upau y anvem korum kosolo
   Deva' martam ulo
   Tum punn Saiba kakultty muj' kornum
   Vor mak' tuj' rajantum

Rorhtam, rorhtam
Duk'm golloitam
Sodanch furhar muz' chintitam

1. Reflecting on my whole life, I move in sorrow. There is no one in the world to console me.

2. This world truly seems a pool of sorrow. There is not one who can tell me that he is happy.

3. From the moment God made me, I was sunk in sorrow. When will I find happiness - only when I am no more?

4. What can I do? I cry out to God. At least you, Lord, have mercy on me, and take me to your kingdom.

I weep and weep, with tears streaming. I always think of my future.

Commentary, p. 152.

Villap 19

LUSITANO RODRIGUES
(+1943)

Soglem mujem vido chintunum

1. Soglem mujem vido chintunum
   Vellu muzo karhtam rorhunum
   Sonsrant maka naim re konnom
   Kallza' muja diucha' buzvonnom

2. E sonsaracha suka' lagunum
   Vido mujem galy'm ibarhunum
   Sonxtam y aum-um tuja pasunum
   Em mujery Devan dal-llam munnum

3. Itlean sonsar naka re maka
   Sonsrach' volloky aili re maka
   Mortrich punnum Devanum maka
   Veleary puro sorgincha suka

   Koslem vido mujem, vido mujem
   Dukantum jieuchem

1. Viewing the whole of my life, I pass my days weeping. There is no one in the world who can comfort my heart.

2. I ruined my life for this world's happiness. For your sake, I suffer it all, because God has sent [this trial] on me.

3. From now on, life will be joyless for me, as I have understood what it means. May God, at least after I die, take me to the joy of heaven.

   What a life mine is, oh, what a life, to live in sadness always !

Commentary, p. 153.

Villap 20

UTÍLCIA REBELO
(1886/7-1960)

Kity'm kon-n sanddun gel' re maka

1. Kity'm kon-n sanddun gel' re maka
   Ily'm punn custar zaly'm nam tuka
   Borem moronn mag re maka
   Compani korum' tuka
   Sorgary Deva' tsoicha' maka

2. Curasanvom mirhmirheanchem
Moga bettoit'm tuj' gunnanko
Koslo y amor mum re amtso
Diamantich' valoratso
Sorgary Devan sagrar kortso

3. Mogache muje mamam
Kitem sangyloly'm maka polle
Ingrat kitea' zaly' mukorhe
Dukany'm bortai muje dolle
Kedonn' pautoly'm y aum tumkorhe

Koxtto tuje chintleary moga
Sonsar maka naka

1. How could you leave me? Did you not find it in the least hard? Pray God that I may die a good death, so that I can keep you company and see God in heaven.

2. I offer my grieving heart to your noble self. Such a love as ours, precious as a diamond it was! May God consecrate it in heaven.

3. My dear mother! Can you remember what you told me? Why have you grown so hard toward me? My eyes fill with tears. When shall I be with you again?

When I think of your agonies, love, I do not want to live.

Commentary, p. 153.

COMMENTARY

1. *Mandos of Union* (Ekvott)

The methodology followed in this volume is the same as that adopted in *Song of Goa: Mandos of Yearning,* particularly in the prologue to the Commentary (p. 179) and in the first three Appendices: Bibliography and Spelling (p. 217), Manuscripts Consulted (p. 220), and Informants (p. 222).

Ekvott 1. DOMINGOS MASCARENHAS (1864-1919) *Sarkeanum kituli tum nitolli*

TESTIMONY TO AUTHORSHIP. Hortência Pinto, daughter of composer.

DATE. 1885, composer's marriage. Hortência Pinto (*MMA*, p. 96).

SOURCE OF SCORE. Ibid.

SOURCE OF TEXT. Ibid.

DEDICATION. Wife of composer, Florentina, married on 1 June 1885.

LITERARY FORM. Monologue mando

THEME. Love and dowry. The bridegroom, unashamedly mercenary, uses the mando to give vent to his feeling of annoyance at the insufficiency of the dowry, and of anger against his mother-in-law. He is also rude to his bride, though he considers her good and beautiful.

LANGUAGE. This is one of the few mandos composed in the Barhdexi dialect. Still, some Saxtti forms have been adopted, such as *kituli* (1a, Barhdexi, *kitli*). Barhdexi forms are the following, with their Saxtti equivalents: *aikolear* (1CHc, *aikileary*); *dor* (2d, *dory*); *muntllearu* (2CHa, *mul-lleari*); *vaitt* (2CHb, *vaxtt*), also the Pramann

Konkani form; as is *khoxi* (2CHc, *foxi*); *ternam* (1CHd, *tedonnom)*; the *u* termination in *tonddu* (2CHd, *tonddo*).

Ekvott 2. MESTRE *JANTU*
Inocenti mujem vido

TESTIMONY TO AUTHORSHIP. Jasmina Miranda (1960).

SOURCE OF SCORE. Marinha Bragança e Carvalho, of Vellsaum/Velção, corrected by Aramita Barreto.

DEDICATION. Wife of the composer Joaquim António (or "Jantu") of Bannali/Benaulim, for their wedding.

MUSICAL FORM. Ternary.

LITERARY FORM. Monologue mando.

POETRY AND MUSIC. One of the most tranquil and beautiful of all marriage mandos.

Ekvott 3. AZAVEDO DINIZ (1860-1907)
Tisri kunvori mum go tum

ALTERNATIVE TITLE. *Ful-lleanlem utoro* (from the mando's third verse) as Utílcia Rebelo began it when she sang it in 1959; the present opening is from *VARMD*, p. 100.

TESTIMONY TO AUTHORSHIP. Utílcia Rebelo, the only person we have been able to find who knew the melody. She also personally knew the composer, Aleixo Francisco Xavier Azavedo Diniz (1860-1907).

DATE. After 1873, when the author reached marriageable age, and probably before 1900. This mando is about his first wife Esmeralda Pimenta; his second one was a Maria Aleluia Rodrigues, who outlived him. Azavedo died in 1907 leaving two young sons.

SOURCE OF SCORE. José Pereira, learnt from Utílcia Rebelo in 1959.

SOURCE OF TEXT. *VARMD*, p. 100.

DEDICATION. To his wife Esmeralda Pimenta (with the pre-Portuguese surname Porob/Prabhu) of Rumborhdem, Kurhtori, for their marriage.

OCCASION. Azavedo's father died young, and the boy was raised by his sister, who also died young. Before her death, she made him promise her three things. First, not to marry into the Porob family; second, not to marry before he had built a hall to their house; and third, not to owe anyone any money. He broke all the three promises, especially the first. He met his first wife Esmeralda at a wedding and fell in love with her at once. She belonged to a family which before the conversion of Saxtty/Salcete to Christianity had borne the surname "Porob". One gathers that Esmeralda was a third daughter (1a), and Azavedo an only son and heir (*morgad*, 1b).

MUSICAL FORM. Ternary.

LITERARY FORM. Monologue mando.

Ekvott 4. ROQUE CORREIA-AFONSO (1859-1937) *Bara tera vorsam zalim*

TESTIMONY TO AUTHORSHIP. Semeão Costa, in *MMA* p. 11. The composer, Roque Correia Afonso was from Bannali/ Benaulim.

DATE. 1892-1893, according to Semeão, in *loc. cit.*

SOURCE OF SCORE. José Maria Borges and Climaco Rodrigues.

SOURCE OF TEXT. *MGC*, p. 26v.

DEDICATION. J. Barreto and Emiliana Correia-Afonso, for their wedding, which took place after 12 years of courtship.

MUSICAL FORM. Ternary.

LITERARY FORM. Monologue mando.

Ekvott 5. ARNALDO DE MENEZES (1863-1917) *Soglem vido mum re mujem*

TESTIMONY TO AUTHORSHIP. Constâncio Lobo, and Praxedes Costa (?).

SOURCE OF SCORE. Rosa Consolação Sequeira, as remembered by her son Micael Martins.

SOURCE OF TEXT. *VARMD*, pp. 59-60. Exceptions: 1c, *amchem*, from *AM* (*VARMD* has *mujem*). CHa has *dileary*, from *AM* (*VARMD* has *mel-lleary*).

DEDICATION. Supposedly for the marriages of Agostinho Colaço and Saturnino Silva. Also, of a lawyer nicknamed "Popai".

MUSICAL FORM. Ternary.

LITERARY FORM. Monologue mando.

POETRY AND MUSIC. One of the most romantic of the mandos of union.

LANGUAGE. *Tokrhi,* old form of *torhi.* We heard an old woman, Alexandrina Pimenta of Rumborhdem, Kurhtori, use it in normal conversation.

Ekvott 6. GIZELINO REBELO (1875-1931)
Diso ekleponnantule

TESTIMONY TO AUTHORSHIP. André Costa, Plácido Costa, Semeão Costa and Utílcia Rebelo. The author, Gizelino Rebelo, is unrivalled as a composer of *ekvott* mandos (though a bachelor himself).

DATE. 1917.

SOURCE OF SCORE. Semeão Costa.

SOURCE OF TEXT. *VARMD,* p. 175.

DEDICATION. Alexandre ("Axu") Diniz, son of the composer Azavedo Diniz (and brother of the compiler of *VARMD*) for his wedding, on 10 February 1917.

MUSICAL FORM. Ternary.

LITERARY FORM. Monologue mando.

ALLUSIONS. 3a. *Papa morun muzo gelo.* Azavedo the composer died on 27 July 1907. 3b. *Retrat punn dekilnam mamantso.* Alexandre was Azavedo's son by his first wife, Esmeralda Pimenta, who died not many years after her marriage some time in the late 19th century (?).

LANGUAGE. 3d. *Aum-um-im.* This double suffix does not, to our knowledge, occur in any other mando. The first suffix is formed by lengthening *aum.* The second, *-im,* means "also". In ordinary conversation, one uses *aum-im/anvuim.*

Ekvott 7. GIZELINO REBELO (1875-1931)
Lanom burgeponnam sanum

ALTERNATIVE TITLE. *Lanom burgeponnim sanum,* as sung by Carmelina Pereira.

TESTIMONY TO AUTHORSHIP. Plácido Costa, Carmelina Pereira and Arsentina Pereira.

SOURCE OF SCORE. José Pereira, learnt from Carmelina Pereira in 1960.

SOURCE OF TEXT. Plácido Costa (1960), who probably got it from the composer himself. See also *VARMD,* pp. 155-156.

VARIANTS. The following variants of Carmelina Pereira are of interest: 1a. *Burgeponnim.* 2a. *axlol'm y aum sorgari.* CH. *Magnnem y amim korya re Devako Feliz y amim zaucha' furharako.*

DEDICATION. The tailor Pedro Sequeira e Melo, for his wedding.

OCCASION. Pedro was an orphan, brought up by a landlord named Melo. The mando (in 1ab and 2a) alludes to his happy childhood. When Pedro grew up and wished to marry, Melo would not consent. Pedro insisted, and was thrown out of Melo's house. The match was arranged by an uncle of Pedro's (3b). Before the wedding, Pedro requested Gizelino to compose this mando, which ends with a hope that the marriage would give him a more secure life.

MUSICAL FORM. Ternary.

LITERARY FORM. Monologue mando.

ALLUSIONS. *Borvons' dovon-n Devacheri Ulas galtam noketranri.* The stars are the cause of evil and God of all good.

Ekvott 8. GIZELINO REBELO (1875-1931) *Nirmit zaunum re Devachem*

TESTIMONY TO AUTHORSHIP. Semeão Costa, Plácido Costa, Utílcia Rebelo and Adolfina Moniz. *Dissent* from Loióla Pacheco (according to Alberto Rodrigues). But Adolfina Moniz's testimony is decisive, as the mando was composed for her.

DATE. 1910.

SOURCE OF SCORE. Semeão Costa.

SOURCE OF TEXT. *METNC*, p. 42.

DEDICATION. Mestre Rosário Moniz and his bride Adolfina, for their wedding in 1910.

MUSICAL FORM. Ternary.

LITERARY FORM. Monologue mando.

Ekvott 9. GIZELINO REBELO (1875-1931) Sontos bogta re jivako Uzvarh petlla e gorako

TESTIMONY TO AUTHORSHIP. Utílcia Rebelo, Semeão Costa and Plácido Costa.

DATE. Between 1887 and 1902, according to Utílcia, and around 1910, according to Semeão.

SOURCE OF SCORE. Rosa Consolação Sequeira, learnt from Mestre Coelho and noted down by Micael Martins before 1923.

SOURCE OF TEXT. *VARMD,* p. 142, with corrections by Semeão. Another version of the text occurs on p. 7 of the same MS, but that page is termite-eaten.

VARIANTS. CHb. *VARMD* has *mogrinantso* instead of *mogureantso.*

DEDICATION. Dr. Meireles Correia and his bride Brazinha (Furtado?), according to Utílcia Rebelo, for their wedding.

MUSICAL FORM. Ternary.

LITERARY FORM. Monologue mando.

ALLUSIONS. 2cd. *Estolacha re pontanum Ekttaim amchem kelem corasaum-om.* Refers to the part of the marriage when the priest places the stole over the joined hands of the couple to stress the sacramental character of the union.

POETRY AND MUSIC. This mando is one of the most popular, and was sung by all classes, as by laborers' wives during weeding and other operations in the fields.

Ekvott 10. GIZELINO REBELO (1875-1931)
Surya sontosan udelo

TESTIMONY TO AUTHORSHIP. Utílcia Rebelo, Semeão Costa, Plácido Costa and Aramita Barreto (?).

DATE. 1927, according to a paper owned by Aramita Barreto(?).

SOURCE OF SCORE. Aramita Barreto (?).

SOURCE OF TEXT. Utílcia Rebelo, in 1960. Also, a loose paper owned by Aramita Barreto.

DEDICATION. Mestre Ambrósio Viegas (son of *Sonar* [goldsmith] Carminho Viegas) and his bride Esmeraldinha, for their wedding.

MUSICAL FORM. Ternary.

LITERARY FORM. Monologue mando.

ALLUSIONS. 1ab. *Surya sontosan udelo Noketranim cercar taka kelo.* The obsession with the imagery of light, a characteristic of the Mando, leads the poet to pile splendors. The expressionistic image of the sun surrounded by the stars and by a halo leads on to that of glow and light of the saints, in which the marriage is sanctified. The latter image seems to be reminiscent of the lines from Psalm 109: 3, *in splendoribus sanctorum, ex utero ante luciferum genui te.*

Ekvott 11. GIZELINO REBELO (1875-1931)
Suryan uzvarhu dampilo

TESTIMONY TO AUTHORSHIP. Semeão Costa, Plácido Costa, and Utílcia Rebelo (?).

SOURCE OF SCORE. Semeão Costa.

SOURCE OF TEXT. *LFMC,* pp. 50-50v. with some changes according to *FXV,* pp. 9-9v. and Plácido Costa.

VARIANTS. 1a. *FXV* has *uzvarh re,* instead of *uzvarhu.* 1b. *LFMC* has *Noketrantso porzoll fankarolo.* 1c. *LFMC* has *Abrilacha satvea munn tea disa,* which, according to Plácido, is quite wrong. 1d. *LFMC* has *Tumtso ekvott sagrar zalo.* 2cd. *FXV* has *Tovoi aji y amim getlo Devan feliz keleary puro.* 4d. *FXV* has *amigam' sanddunaka.* CHb. *FXV* has *prosperar,* instead of *conservar.*

MUSICAL FORM. Ternary.

LITERARY FORM. Monologue mando.

ALLUSIONS. *Gumgumm zoborh yeta re tsampeantso.* The *tsampem* or *champaka,* one of the flowers beloved of Sanskrit poets, is known in botany as *plumeria acutifolia/acuminata.* The older name was *Michelia champaca.*

Ekvott 12. TORQUATO DE FIGUEIREDO (1876-1948)
Derfente uzvarh fankarolo

TESTIMONY TO AUTHORSHIP. Constâncio Lobo, João Medeira, Abelardo Valadares and Elizena Vaz, all acquaintances of the composer.

DATE. 1918-1919, according to Joaquim and João Medeira.

SOURCE OF SCORE. Padre Enrique Medeira.

SOURCE OF TEXT. Elizena Vaz (21 July 1957).

DEDICATION. Ricarda Medeira of Lotlli/Loutulim and António Rodrigues of Kurhtori/Curtorim, for their wedding.

MUSICAL FORM. Ternary.

LITERARY FORM. Monologue mando.

LANGUAGE. 1a. *Derfente,* from Portuguese, *de repente.*

Ekvott 13. TORQUATO DE FIGUEIREDO (1876-1948)
Sontos bogta re jivako Ekvott y aji zala munnum y amtso

TESTIMONY TO AUTHORSHIP. Elizena Vaz (21 January 1957), Maria Figueiredo e Mesquita (1960), Abelardo Valadares (1960) and *MFM,* p. 7.

SOURCE OF SCORE. Elizena Vaz (1957).
SOURCE OF TEXT. *MFM, loc. cit.*
MUSICAL FORM. Ternary.
LITERARY FORM. Monologue mando.

Ekvott 14. TORQUATO DE FIGUEIREDO (1876-1948)
Suryan uzvarh fankarolo

TESTIMONY TO AUTHORSHIP. Roque Menezes (who assisted in the mando's composition) and Abelardo Valadares.

DATE. 1940.

SOURCE OF SCORE. Roque Menezes (1954). Published in *Marg*.

SOURCE OF TEXT. *Ibid.*

DEDICATION. Riário Moniz and Helena Quadros, for their wedding in 1940.

OCCASION. The bridegroom Riário was from Kurhtori/ Curtorim, and the bride Helena from Morhgoum/Margão. Their elders met to arrange the match, but the bride's mother died while the talks were going on (2d). The uncle settled the match, but he died soon after of cancer of the stomach (2abc). Three months after his death Riário and Helena were married.

CIRCUMSTANCES OF COMPOSITION. Composed in Torquato's house (in the veranda?) with the assistance of Dr. Roque Menezes. In 2a, Torquato intended to write *Nimann dezej [desejo] tuj' tivatso,* but on Dr. Menezes's suggestion, replaced the Portuguese word with the Konkani *visvas*. The doctor himself narrated this anecdote.

MUSICAL FORM. Ternary.

LITERARY FORM. Monologue mando.

Ekvott 15. PASCOAL NORONHA (1872-1936)
Paicha maincha moreantulim

TESTIMONY TO AUTHORSHIP. *PFBN* (the composer's book of his own mandos), Artemísia Melo, Roque Menezes, and Mrs. António Pacheco.

DATE. 1925, according to *AB*, p. 142.

SOURCE OF SCORE. Luzia Medeira e Rosário.

SOURCE OF TEXT. Original, *PFBN*, pp. 7-8 (with changes in orthography).

DEDICATION. "De uma noiva em dia do seu casamento," *PFBN, loc. cit.* Three possible identifications: Geneviva Dias e Cruz, according to Dr. Roque Menezes; Bemvinda, according to *AB*, p. 142; Mrs. António Pacheco; or Luzia Medeira herself.

MUSICAL FORM. Binary.

LITERARY FORM. Monologue mando.

ALLUSIONS. 2ab.*Tsoliant poilem y aum-um follo Paich'-mainch y asa maka bollo.* The belief is that as the age of the parents increases, so lessens their vigor and that of the children born to them.

Ekvott 16. PASCOAL NORONHA (1872-1936)
Amcha gorchanche foxenum

ALTERNATIVE TITLE. *Amcha vorhanche foxenum.*

TESTIMONY TO AUTHORSHIP. *PFBN*, pp. 40-41. Corroboration by Roque Menezes (1954) and Artemísia Melo (1954), and general consensus. *Dissent* from Julieta Colaço (1954), who believes it to be the work of the composer's rival Joaquim Santana Menezes.

DATE. 1929, *PFBN, loc. cit.*

SOURCE OF SCORE. Artemísia Melo, with corrections by Luzia Medeira.

SOURCE OF TEXT. Original. *PFBN, loc. cit.*

DEDICATION. Daughter of Agostinho Quadros, for her wedding, according to *op. cit., loc. cit.*

MUSICAL FORM. Binary.

LITERARY FORM. Monologue mando.

ALLUSIONS. *Bangrach' daiek Adar unttitso,* a Konkani proverb.

POETRY. Pascoal's mandos are perhaps the most moralizing of all those in existence, compendia of maxims for those about to be married.

Ekvott 17. JOAQUIM SANTANA MENEZES (1898-1939)
Sodanch chintitalim y aum-um

TESTIMONY TO AUTHORSHIP. Francisco Xavier Colaço, Julieta Colaço, Plácido Costa and Carmelina Pereira (?).

DATE. 1922-1923, according to *MMA*, p. 83.

SOURCE OF SCORE. Rubertina Costa and Aninhas Costa Cardoso.

SOURCE OF TEXT. Carmelina Pereira, with corrections by

Rubertina Costa.

DEDICATION. Margarida Correia Afonso of Bannali/ Benaulim and Dr. Peregrino da Costa of Aquem, for their wedding, according to Agapito Miranda. It was also sung at the wedding of Juliema Bonaparte, according to Julieta Colaço.

ANECDOTES IN THE HISTORY OF THE SONG. Peregrino, the suitor, a noted physician, was a Shudra, and his bride-to-be Margarida, a Brahmin. Her father, who greatly admired Peregrino, overcame his caste prejudice, and himself proposed that they be married. It is said that he sang the mando in his sedan chair all the way to the prospective bridegroom's house where he was being taken to convey the proposal of marriage.

MUSICAL FORM. Ternary.

LITERARY FORM. Monologue mando.

THEME. A Brahmin girl marries outside caste, and oscillates between loyalty to caste (vv. 1-2) and more liberal ideas (v. 3). There is irony in the verse that shows her final acceptance of the liberal viewpoint.

Ekvott 18. FRANCISCO SARDINHA (1897-1958) *Aji pasun Devachery patyeunum*

TESTIMONY TO AUTHORSHIP. Roque Menezes (1954) and Emília Araújo (1960).

SOURCE OF SCORE. Roque Menezes, in September 1962.

SOURCE OF TEXT. Emília Araújo, September 1962.

DEDICATION. Emília Araújo, for her wedding.

MUSICAL FORM. Ternary.

LITERARY FORM. Monologue mando.

POETRY AND MUSIC. 1cd. *Sorgim' surya' noketram' tsounum Vellu muzo passar kortaly'm aum-um.* The theme of the lovers gazing at the celestial luminaries, while thinking of their loved ones, recurs frequently in the mando. See v. 3 of *Tuzo mogu mum re anja* (*Utrike* 39) and v. 3 of *Vintsun karhilolea suka* (*Utrike* 29).

2. *Mandos of Lamentation* (Villap)

Villap 1. LUÍS MENEZES (1866-1936)
Sonsar charich re disantso

TESTIMONY TO AUTHORSHIP. Nicolau Menezes, son of the composer. General consensus. The opinion has been expressed that the reputed author, Luís Manuel Menezes (1866-1936), may have got the mando composed, at least as regards the melody, by a professional musician.

DATE. Before 1895, the date of the composer's marriage, and after 1879, when he attained the age of puberty.

SOURCE OF SCORE. John Athaíde, an undetermined MS, or *ASMM*, p. 22.

SOURCE OF TEXT. *AB*, pp. 64-65 (for vv. 1, 2, 4, & 5) and *ASMM, loc. cit.,* (for v. 3).

DEDICATION. Maria Aninha, who jilted the composer and then married another man.

ANECDOTES IN THE HISTORY OF THE SONG. Maria Aninha, coming out of the church after her wedding, saw Luís waiting for her at the door. There he started to sing this mando, accusing her in public of faithlessness. This episode is similar to that of Adolfinho singing Arnaldo's *Tuzo mogu axlol' munnum* (see *Villap* 8). In making such a dramatic public statement, Adolfinho may have been inspired by Luís's example.

MUSICAL FORM. Binary.

LITERARY FORM. Monologue mando.

ALLUSIONS. 2c. *Kallyza' bale marnum satu Marianinh.* Seven swords pierced the heart of the Virgin. The image of the Madonna, her heart aureoled by seven piercing swords, is popular in Goan, as in Iberian, art.

Villap 2. ANAMU/ANONYMOUS
Maingeri paigeri

ALTERNATIVE TITLE. *Paigeri maingeri.*

TESTIMONY TO AUTHORSHIP. Jasmina Miranda told us

that she knew the name of the composer (a Lotllykar), though she had at the moment forgotten it. She said that she would soon recall it, but one of us who interviewed her (Pereira) never saw her again.

AFFILIATION. Lotlli.

SOURCE OF SCORE. José Pereira, learnt from Carmelina Pereira, in 1960.

SOURCE OF TEXT. Carmelina Pereira, 1960 (for vv. 1, 2, 3ab) and *LFMC* p. 10 (for v. 3).

VARIANTS. 1a. *LFMC Paigeri maingeri*. 1c. *LFMC* omits *Ai*. 1d. *LFMC has Bagem kituly'm instead* of *Bagi kituly'*. 2c. *LFMC* has *ya* instead of *ai*. 3a. *LFMC* has *Muzo pai anim maim-im*, instead of *Maim-im y anim pai-i*.

MUSICAL FORM. Binary.

LITERARY FORM. Monologue mando.

THEME. One daughter among many sons, the elder of whom has some money. But the family is poor, with no money for the daughter's dowry.

Villap 3. ANAMU/ANONYMOUS
Zaite sukanum varholim

AFFILIATION. Kurhtori.

SOURCE OF SCORE. José Pereira, learnt from Carmelina Pereira in 1960.

SOURCE OF TEXT. Carmelina Pereira (11 October 1960).

VARIANTS. Carmelina repeats 3ab twice, to form four lines-as if 3ab were 3abcd. It is difficult to say if this was really the composer's intention, or just forgetfulness on Carmelina's part, probably the latter.

DEDICATION. Fielzinha da Costa of Batorhem, Kurhtori/ Curtorim.

MUSICAL FORM. Binary.

LITERARY FORM. Dialogue mando.

Villap 4. PAULO MILAGRES SILVA (1855-1931)
Tsondrimm kupam' fankarolo

ALTERNATIVE TITLE. *Mujem vido cabar kelem;* also, *Soglem vido ibarhilem*, the first verse of *MGC*, p. 10.

TESTIMONY TO AUTHORSHIP. Semeão Costa, Filipe Costa and Jasmina Miranda (?).

SOURCE OF SCORE. Semeão Costa.

SOURCE OF TEXT. *MGC*, p. 10, with some corrections from *AB*, p. 26. As advised by Semeão, we have taken the second verse of *MGC* as our first.

VARIANTS. 1c. *MGC lagun re*. 2a. *MGC Soglem vido ibarhilem*. 2b. *MGC re* omitted after *moga*. 3a. *AB, sarkem dekun tujem*, instead of *tujem tsounum* (*MGC*). 3c. *MGC Tuj' lagy'm cazar mum go zaunum*. 3d. *AB bogytal'm y axlol'm y aum-um*.

MUSICAL FORM. Ternary.

LITERARY FORM. Monologue mando.

Villap 5. ANAMU/ANONYMOUS
Ek dis bagint y aum gelolim

AFFILIATION. Barhdes.

SOURCE OF SCORE. Joaquim Furtado of Ol-lli/Orlim.

SOURCE OF TEXT. From a loose sheet, written by an anonymous writer several years ago, in possession of José Pereira.

DEDICATION. Ernesto (v. 3).

MUSICAL FORM. Ternary.

LITERARY FORM. Monologue mando.

THEME. A young man shows interest in a girl, but she is too shy to encourage him. Later, she laments that she thus lost the man she could have married.

POETRY AND MUSIC. "Perhaps greater than the pain of being betrayed after having been once loved is the pain of never having loved at all. And greater than even this is the pain of having let slip the one and only chance which might have... oh, the pain of the thought that she had only to have said the word, and...

This is the theme of one of the most poignant mandos. A masterpiece in the art of suggestion, a song in which the pathos of an old maid's life is so gently and quietly conveyed. She was young and beautiful. One day, walking from her garden to her home, with a few abolim in her hand, she met a young man, and, strangely enough, he asked for the flowers. Why should a young man want flowers? Who is there in his home to wear flowers? Perhaps no one. Even at the moment of giving them to him, 'two words' flitted across her mind. But her lips never formed them into sounds. If only she had 'spoken' them, her life would have been a different one. Today she is a lonely old maid, hungering for love and marriage". Lucio

Rodrigues, "Folk Songs of Goa. 1. Mando - The Song of Love," *Journal of the University of Bombay* (January 1954), p. 75.

LANGUAGE. This song is in the northern dialect of Barhdexi, and not in the standard dialect of the mando, Saxtti. In Barhdexi, the *u* and *o* terminations for nouns are not used in the colloquial and written language, and are often omitted in poetry. In Saxtti, the *u* is a masculine termination (as in *munisu*, "man"), the *o* either feminine or neuter (as in *bailo*, "woman," and *dukoro*, "pig"). When Barhdexi uses any terminations at all, in song and poetry, it employs *u* without any distinction of gender (*munisu, bailu, dukoru*, etc.).

Unlike Saxtti, Barhdexi does not employ elision. 2a in Saxtti would have been as follows: *Aboly'm ditonn'm y aum-um rol-llim,* in the normal mando rhythm, of two anapests and trochee. The same line in Barhdexi is *Abolim ditannam aum rol-llim*, which does not scan properly. Among other differences between the two dialects is that Saxtti uses the semivowel y (*kory*, "do"), which Barhdexi does not (*kor*).

The text, as it now stands, is a hybrid of Barhdexi and Saxtti. In its original version, the first verse and chorus probably read as follows:

Ek dis bagint aum gelelim Torhim getlim anvem abolim Tinvim aum geun yetalim Eka tsolean magun velim. Faleam aum abolim arhtelim Tuka ditelim Tumger gara konnum asat re Fulam mautelim.

Villap 6. CÉSAR-MENDES
Dony-tinim muinnem zale muj' moga

ALTERNATIVE TITLE. *Dony-tinim muinnem zale Mary'-Elen* (Maria Helena).

TESTIMONY TO AUTHORSHIP. Aleixo Costa.

DATE. 1890-1900, according to Semeão Costa.

SOURCE OF SCORE. Ibid.

SOURCE OF TEXT. *FXV*, p. 39v., with some corrections by Semeão. He rearranges the order of the verses of *FXV* as follows: 1-3-4-5-6-2-7-8. We follow that order.

VARIANTS. We have accepted the following corrections of the *FXV* text by Semeão: 1a. *muinnem*, instead of *diso*. 5e. *suicidar*, instead of *cazaro*. 6d. *munn go moga*, instead of *muja moga*. 9d. *dispidiro*, instead of *respondero*.

DEDICATION. Maria Helena, who later married César Pinho.

OCCASION. The mando tells its own story of the author's love for Maria Helena. The young man's parents were against his marrying her, and first tried to get him made a priest (v. 8), and then got him a post in the police force (which frequently employed mestizos like the author). He tried to keep in touch with the girl through letters, sent through a friend, César Pinho, who not only betrayed his trust, but later himself married Maria. This unbalanced the lover completely. His duty as a policeman was to stand guard at the door of the Governor's palace at Ponnji/Panaji/Panjim. One morning he blew his brains out with his pistol while at his post.

Though a mestizo, belonging to a group that boasted about its Portuguese ancestry, the unfortunate youth knew Konkani well; it was customary for many mestizo families to speak Konkani at home. Very few songs were composed in Portuguese; Konkani had become the general medium of songs (including those with political content) from the 1850s. However, there are other people who think that César Mendes may have got his mando composed by another musician. The intensity of the feeling expressed in the mando makes it unlikely.

MUSICAL FORM. Binary.

LITERARY FORM. Monologue mando.

Villap 7. ARNALDO DE MENEZES (1863-1917)
Ai kitem y anvem korchem

TESTIMONY TO AUTHORSHIP. Semeão Costa and Artemísia Melo.

DATE. Between 1912 and 1914, according to Semeão.

SOURCE OF SCORE. Plácido Costa, 1960.

SOURCE OF TEXT. *VARMD*, p. 161.

VARIANTS.2b. *atich'm*, substituted for the Bambonn Saxtti form *atach'm/atachim*.

DEDICATION. Edviges Costa.

MUSICAL FORM. Ternary.

LITERARY FORM. Monologue mando.

THEME. Lament on the premature death of a beloved husband.

ALLUSIONS. 2b. *Atach'm kanknnam mujim fol-llim.* At the death of her husband, the Hindu widow broke her bangles and removed all her jewelry and ornaments. The Christian descendants of the Hindus continued this custom.

LANGUAGE. 2b. *Atach'm* (Brahmin form), instead of *atich'm* (Tsad-ddi and Shudra form). The mando uses Brahmin Saxtti as its main dialect. There is no evidence that the woman in this mando was not a Brahmin; we changed the word to the Brahmin form.

Villap 8. ARNALDO DE MENEZES (1863-1917) The Adolfinian Trilogy, 1 *Tuzo mogu axlol' munnum*

TESTIMONY TO AUTHORSHIP. Semeão Costa, Plácido Costa, and Dr. Gambeta Costa (a nephew of Adolfinho), who is absolutely positive. Bráulio Carvalho and Roque Menezes (in 1954) dissented. But later Roque admitted that he might have been mistaken, and that Arnaldo (not Adolfinho himself) was probably the composer.

DATE. Around 1901, sometime before the wedding of Maria Adelina da Costa and Vicente Barbosa, which took place on 19 April 1901.

SOURCE OF SCORE. Semeão Costa.

SOURCE OF TEXT. *VARMD*, pp. 77-78, with some corrections from *AB*, p.115. Also, text by Semeão, published *Marg, loc. cit.*, p. 65, and with further changes in *Goan Tribune* of 10 February 1957, p. 8.

VARIANTS. 1ab. Semeão: *Tuzo mogu maka munnum Porgottola sogloch gaum-um.*

1c. *VARMD*: *kallyzant gutto.*

2CHa. Semeão: *atam* omitted after *kallizache*. 2CHa. *VARMD*: *sintment re muje*; *AB*: *sintimento muje*. We feel that this practice of joining a suffix to a preceding word, instead of placing *re* after it, is a more sophisticated one, and is followed by *VARMD* in 3CHa *vollvolle muje* (instead of *vollvolly' re muje*). *Re*, we believe, is best employed when the preceding word can have no suffix, such as in 1CHa, *gave re muje*, and 4CHa, *vallo re muje.*

2b. Semeão: *Dusreach' keli munnum y axi.* Verse 3. Semeão: omitted. 3a. *VARMD*: *pixi* instead of *AB*'s *tontti*; *tontti* rhymes better with *fatti, fotti and valtti*, and omits the repetition of *pixi* (found in 2a) in a similar context.

4b. VARMD: *Kitea' sanddun gely' re maka*, while Semeão and Artemísia Melo have *Kity'm kon-n sanddun vot' re maka*. We feel that *vota* is more appropriate than *geli* for the occasion at which the mando was sung. At that moment, the marriage ceremony, which would forever separate Adelina and Adolfinho, was being performed, and Adelina was in truth renouncing him for good.

4c. Semeão: *Soglem vido,* instead of *Mujem vido; VARMD*: *anja,* instead of *mannyka* (*AB*), which rhymes better with the preceding line.

DEDICATION. Maria Adelina da Costa.

OCCASION AND CIRCUMSTANCES OF COMPOSITION. A friend of Arnaldo's, Adolfo da Piedade Costa, or Adolfinho (1864-1914), a clerk at the Fazenda, Morhgoum/Margão, was deeply in love with a girl named Maria Adelina da Costa, perhaps a near relative. Adolfinho was a clever and educated man, but with little money, and it is doubtful if Adelina ever loved him. When shopping in the New Market (Mercado Novo, Novem Bazar) one day, Arnaldo met him by chance: Adolfinho was looking desperately unhappy, and was sighing without restraint (*Ai! ai!*). Arnaldo asked him the reason of his grief, and was told that Adelina was to be married to another man, a Vicente Caetano Santana Barbosa, of the *Erondd* family, 37 years of age, older than the bride by 17 years. Arnaldo decided to help his friend make his grief public in a dramatic way.

The bride was getting ready for the ceremony on the wedding morning, and Adolfinho was out in the rain, kneeling in the mud, crying out to her, begging her to change her mind while there was still time. She ignored him, and he followed her to the church (Morhgoum, Espírito Santo). As the wedding was being celebrated, as was the custom then, at the church door, Adolfinho lay down on the raised platform of steps in front of it, his arms stretched out in the form of a cross, and made his last appeal in song to his beloved Adelina, through the mando that Arnaldo had composed for him. The wedding went on, nevertheless, and Adolfinho, destroyed, died an alcoholic in 1914.

MUSICAL FORM. Ternary.

LITERARY FORM. Monologue mando.

ALLUSIONS. To Christ's crucifixion. 1cd. *Kallyzach' gutto tuje mujery dovon-num Y atam morum' paulam y aum-um.* "He was bearing our faults in his own body on the cross, so that we might die to our faults and live for holiness; through his wounds you have been healed" (I Peter 2: 24). "And yet ours were the sufferings he bore, ours the sorrows he carried. But we thought of him as someone punished, struck by God, and brought low" (Isaiah 53: 4).

1CHa. *Ai, ai, ontoskornanche gave re muje.* Apparently a reference to the piercing of Christ's side with a lance.

2cd. *Tuje mainko zoborhy zoborhy zaly' foxi Enddeach' ruka' fursary marchi. Erondd* (nominative of *enddeach'*) is the physic nut tree or *Jathropa curcas*. It was the nickname of the Barbosa family of Morhgoum into which Adelina married.

3c. *Camilacho tumim aikunum fotti.* The identity of this Camilo is unknown; evidently an enemy of Adolfinho's who poisoned the minds of the Barbosas against Adolfinho.

3d. *Maka eucha' pauli valtti.* In Konkani idiom, to be attacked by termites, is for a man to lose his inner substance, outlive his usefulness, be finished, demoralized, and become a spent force.

POETRY AND MUSIC. This Trilogy is among the most tragic numbers of the Mando; two aspects can be distinguished in it, the moods and the motifs.

The *moods*, in their transitions from one to another, unite the members of the Trilogy. In the first member, *Tuzo mogu axlol' munnum*, the pain at the separation is excruciating and affirms itself with violent insistence. In the second member, *Motim' sopnnantum naxlolem*, the sense of loss is still fresh, but in the third, *Chintun furhar Deva muzo*, despair yields to a resignation not of this world.

As for the *motifs*, no single one runs through the three mandos. The main theme is symbolically that of the Crucifixion, and in the first mando, the lover's sufferings are delineated in terms of Christ's agony on the cross. An explicit reference to this sacred event is found in 2d, and there are other lines that recall the Passion story, where Jesus dies burdened with our sorrows (echoed in 1cd) and pierced in His heart (cf. ICH). But the Crucifixion is not fully paralleled by the lover's agony, for, while the pain and consummated suffering of Christ terminate at the Resurrection, the anguish and betrayal of the lover end in an irrevocable loss. The Crucifixion motif fades out in the second member of the Trilogy but reappears in the third, in its last verse, which depicts the sun hidden behind clouds, suggesting the dark hours of Calvary.

To state the moods in terms of the motif, *Tuzo mogu maka munnum* throbs with the emotions associated with the Crucifixion (in its imagery); *Motim' sopnnantum naxlolem* evokes the mood of the Taking Down from the Cross and the Procession to the Tomb (cf. v. 4), and *Chintun furhar Deva muzo* embodies the spirit of the Entombment in its fatal melancholy and resignation.

Villap 9. ARNALDO DE MENEZES (1863-1917) The Adolfinian Trilogy, 2. *Motim' sopnnantum naxlolem*

TESTIMONY TO AUTHORSHIP. Semeão Costa, Plácido Costa, Dr. Gambeta Costa and Ezilda Barreto e Menezes (Arnaldo's widow). General consensus. Roque Menezes, in 1954, believed it to have been the work of Adolfinho himself. But in that same year, Dr. Gambeta Costa informed us that his uncle (Adolfinho) had got Arnaldo to compose it. Arnaldo's wife corroborated this view, also in 1954; in fact, she told us how the mando was composed (see CIRCUMSTANCES OF COMPOSITION, below). Informed of these opinions, Roque Menezes confessed that he could have been wrong. But Bráulio Carvalho persisted in his view that Adolfinho was the author.

DATE. As Adelina's wedding took place in 1901, this mando must be of approximately the same date.

SOURCE OF SCORE. Semeão, published in *Marg, loc. cit.*, p. 66.

SOURCE OF TEXT. *VARMD*, pp. 55-56, with some corrections by Semeão; also, *AB*, p. 113

VARIANTS. 1a. *VARMD*: *Motintum sopnnam' naxlolem.*

1b. Semeão: *Deva dizgras mujery ailem.*

1CHa. Semeão: *Sonsrach' axa sanddily' re moga.*

v. 3. Semeão: omitted.

4CHb. *VARMD*: *Adeus Adclina muja anja*; Semeão: *muja moga.*

DEDICATION. Adolfo/Adolfinho da Piedade Costa and Maria Adelina da Costa.

CIRCUMSTANCES OF COMPOSITION. Arnaldo and his wife Ezilda were on their way one morning to Morhgoum in a horse-drawn carriage, when they sighted Adolfinho walking toward them, motioning them to stop. He wanted a mando, and obliged Arnaldo to go back with him to Kurhtori to compose it. Ezilda recalled the two men discussing the mando in the hall (destroyed) of the composer's house, with Arnaldo singing (composing?) it, and Adolfinho suggesting changes.

ANECDOTES IN THE HISTORY OF THE SONG. Bráulio Carvalho says that Adolfinho sang this mando on the steps outside the house where Adelina's reception was being held, on the return of the wedded pair and their guests from church. Passers-by also used to see him sing the mando, the tears streaming from his eyes, from the veranda of his house at Morhgoum, which adjoins that of his deceased nephew Dr. Gambeta Costa.

MUSICAL FORM. Ternary.

LITERARY FORM. Monologue mando.

Villap 10. ARNALDO DE MENEZES (1863-1917) The Adolfinian Trilogy, 3. *Chintun furhar Deva muzo*

TESTIMONY TO AUTHORSHIP. General consensus. Semeão Costa, Ezilda Barreto, Aninha Rangel, Plácido Costa, all of whom knew the composer well. *CFF*, p. 11v (written testimony to Arnaldo's authorship in the compiler's hand). Roque Menezes initially believed it to be the work of Adolfinho himself.

DATE. Before 1902, when it was published in Lisbon, unacknowledged, under the title "Dolente," by the composer Carlos Eugénio Ferreira.

SOURCE OF SCORE. Semeão, published in *Marg, loc. cit.*, p. 67.

SOURCE OF TEXT. *VARMD*, pp. 56-57. See also *AB*, p. 112 (vv. 1-3).

VARIANTS. v. 4. *AB*: omitted, either intentionally or through ignorance.

DEDICATION. Originally written by Arnaldo for himself, it was later "appropriated" by Adolfinho, who sang it as if it had been composed for his own predicament.

MUSICAL FORM. Ternary.

LITERARY FORM. Monologue mando.

ALLUSIONS. 4ab. *E muj' dukancha tempari Vellanum keli re molbotti.* Reference to the darkening of the sky at the Crucifixion: "with the sun eclipsed, a darkness came over the whole land until the ninth hour" (Luke 23: 44).

LANGUAGE. 1cd: *gunnan-Ko y anim.* This split within a word, with one part of it carried over into the next verse, common in Kannada poetry, is to our knowledge unique in Konkani Song. Not all versions of our mando have it, but only *VARMD* and Semeão. António Sequeira gives the following alternative reading: *Bou kon-n vellacha gunnanko Anim te nixttur noketranko.*

4d. *kakultty,* the old form of *kakutty* (or *kakutt,* sometimes *kaklutt* in Barhdexi), from the Kannada *kakulatte,* "mercy".

Villap 11. ARNALDO DE MENEZES (1863-1917)
Sintment varoily' e sonsrako

TESTIMONY TO AUTHORSHIP. Wenceslau Soares (1960), who has no doubt about the authorship. Semeão told us how Gizelino Rebelo loved this mando and used to say that he wished that he had composed it himself.

SOURCE OF SCORE. Aninhas Costa Cardoso.

SOURCE OF TEXT. *VARMD*, pp. 158-159.

DEDICATION. Semeão told us the name of this unhappy couple to whom this mando was dedicated, but we missed writing it down, and cannot recall it.

MUSICAL FORM. Ternary.

LITERARY FORM. Monologue mando.

Villap 12. ARNALDO DE MENEZES (1863-1917)
Soglem vido mujem tsounum

ALTERNATIVE TITLE. *Sonsrach' volloky aili maka*, from the mando's second verse, as published in *Marg, loc. cit.*, p. 68.

TESTIMONY TO AUTHORSHIP. *CFF*, pp. 9-10, and Semeão.

SOURCE OF SCORE. Semeão Costa and Caetano Diniz (*SCCD*, VII) apparently corrected by Aramita Barreto. A version of Semeão's was published in *Marg, loc. cit.*

SOURCE OF TEXT. *VARMD*, pp. 51-52, with corrections by Semeão.

VARIANTS. CH. *VARMD*: *soglem vido*, instead of *soglem Deva*.

DEDICATION. Perhaps Idalfo Menezes, Arnaldo's unfriendly neighbor.

MUSICAL FORM. Ternary.

LITERARY FORM. Monologue mando.

ALLUSIONS. 4d. *Sorginch' paundde tsot-ttam y aum-um*. This could be a reference to the ladder of heaven, with angels ascending and descending, which Jacob saw in his dream (*Genesis* 28: 12).

Villap 13. ARNALDO DE MENEZES (1863-1917)
Oromb nuim re y amcha Gointso

TESTIMONY TO AUTHORSHIP. *CFF* (on pp. 24v.-25r), Semeão Costa and Artemisia Melo.

DATE. 1906, according to *CFF*, p. 25r.

SOURCE OF SCORE. Semeão Costa.

SOURCE OF TEXT. *VARMD*, pp. 81-82, with some corrections by Semeão.

VARIANTS. 1c. *VARMD*: *re konnantso,* instead of *nuim konnantso*

DEDICATION. Idalfo Menezes, Arnaldo's neighbor, who was on bad terms with the composer.

MUSICAL FORM. Ternary.

LITERARY FORM. Monologue mando.

THEME. The Goan love of intrigue and and malicious gossip. As an accurate portrayal of a fundamental trait in his people, Arnaldo's mando has no equal.

ALLUSIONS. 2CHab. *Bexttech fobro kelolei tunvem Te tempantum.* This probably refers to some past slander of Idalfo's.

3CHab. *Boguch'm axloly'm boglem tuka Tsoinak'maka.* The poet makes as if Idalfo were staring angrily at him after hearing his criticisms.

Villap 14. GIZELINO REBELO (1875-1931)
Koslem vido mum re y amchem

TESTIMONY TO AUTHORSHIP. Plácido Costa and Utílcia Rebelo, who are positive. Semeão believed it to be Arnaldo's in 1954, but hesitated when told of Plácido's and Utílcia's opinion.

SOURCE OF SCORE. Semeão Costa.

SOURCE OF TEXT. *VARMD*, pp. 60-61; also *AB*, p. 205.

DEDICATION. To a woman whom Gizelino wished to marry. The first two verses describe the misery caused by his hopeless love, and the last, the common sorrow of composer and the woman (according to Bráulio Carvalho).

MUSICAL FORM. Ternary.

LITERARY FORM. Monologue mando.

Villap 15. GIZELINO REBELO (1875-1931)
Chintun caba' korum' nuzo

TESTIMONY TO AUTHORSHIP. Plácido Costa and Utílcia Rebelo, both positive. Semeão first thought that the mando was Arnaldo's, but when confronted with Plácido's and Utílcia's testimony, admitted that he could have been wrong. The similarity of their styles sometimes makes their compositions hard to distinguish.

DATE. Utílcia told us that it was composed before her wedding. We do not know the date of this event, but her husband died in 1932.

SOURCE OF SCORE. Bráulio Carvalho (1959)

SOURCE OF TEXT. *VARMD*, p. 19.

VARIANTS. *VARMD*: *tea kallyzako*. It is more correct to say *te*, as the particle ought to refer to *mirhmirhe*, and not *kallyzako*.

OCCASION. Domestic troubles of Gizelino, described under OCCASION of *Foxalborit bountai y amim* (*Villap 17*).

MUSICAL FORM. Ternary.

LITERARY FORM. Monologue mando.

LANGUAGE. 3d. *Tsoicha' vocha' nimannea garantum*. *Nimannem gor*, "the last house," is death, like all dwelling places a stable nucleus of one's existence, but not changeable, like the others.

Villap 16. GIZELINO REBELO (1875-1931)
Kakultty tsoiyai tumim muji

TESTIMONY TO AUTHORSHIP. Semeão Costa, André Costa, Plácido Costa, Walberga Costa, Utílcia Rebelo and Aramita Barreto, who thinks it to be Gizelino's last mando.

DATE. 1925 or 1928, according to *MMA*, p. 77.

SOURCE OF SCORE. Aninhas Costa Cardoso.

SOURCE OF TEXT. *WC*, p. 31.

VARIANTS. 1b. *WC*: *emkonddachi*, which does not fit the score. The reading, which we adopt, *dukacha konddachi*, is from an uncertain source, probably Aninhas.

MUSICAL FORM. Ternary.

LITERARY FORM. Monologue mando.

Villap 17. GIZELINO REBELO (1875-1931)
Foxalborit bountai y amim

TESTIMONY TO AUTHORSHIP. Semeão Costa and Utílcia Rebelo.

DATE. According to Semeão, about 1916-1918.

SOURCE OF SCORE. Plácido Costa.

SOURCE OF TEXT. *VARMD*, pp. 91-92 (text), *& LFMC*, p. 152 (order of verses). Order of verses in *VARMD*: 1+1CH–2CH+2CH–4+3CH–3+4CH.

OCCASION. Gizelino's father who died while he was yet a boy, left his children in the care of their aunt Amélia, a hard, cruel woman, who used to ill-treat and starve them. Her husband (who was said to have been impotent), later wished to get Gizelino married, but Amélia, who had a lover (her sister-in-law's son, José), threatened to leave the house by the back door the moment Gizelino's bride came in by the front door. Amélia evidently wanted to have as few people as possible in the house, so that she could have privacy with her lover. It is said that she had two children by José, both of whom she is believed to have killed, one by poison and the other by drowning. She was a quarrelsome woman, and had rows with many people, one of them the wife of a Tertuliano, apparently a near relative, which added to Gizelino's misery. The domestic nightmare created by this woman's behavior was the occasion for our mando.

MUSICAL FORM. Ternary.

LITERARY FORM. Monologue mando.

POETRY AND MUSIC. Textually one of the most original mandos. No other mando equals the brilliant irony of its first verses, and their contrast with the passionate explosion in the last verse is unique.

Villap 18. TORQUATO DE FIGUEIREDO (1876-1948) *Soglem mujem vido chintunum Dukan bountam y aum-um*

TESTIMONY TO AUTHORSHIP. Maestro António de Figueiredo, nephew of the composer, wrote a letter to José Pereira on 9 November 1955, where he declared: "...o mandó [é] do meu parente Torcato de Figueiredo. O original que nos foi oferecido pelo autor perdeu-se e eu agora servi-me duma cópia que eu possuo datada de 1918". In addition, Maria Figueiredo e Mesquita, a pupil of Torquato's, Constâncio Lobo, Roque Menezes, Abelardo Valadares and Elizena Vaz (all acquaintances of the composer), testify to Torquato's authorship of this song.

DATE. Before 1918.

SOURCE OF SCORE. Roque Menezes (1954).

SOURCE OF TEXT. From a copy of the original in possession of Maestro António de Figueiredo, dated 1918. Roque Menezes's version was published in *Marg, loc. cit.*, p. 77.

OCCASION. Probably Torquato's frustrated love affair while he was a tutor at Bannali/Benaulim, which is the theme of the mando of yearning *Kedim' chintily'm naim re anvem* (*Utrike* 34).

MUSICAL FORM. Ternary irregular.

LITERARY FORM. Monologue mando.

ALLUSIONS. Of the mando's three allusions, two appear to be biblical:

1bc. *Sonsram' maka nam re konnom Diucha' buzavonnom.* Reminiscent of Psalm 68: 20a: "My shame and disgrace are past cure; I had hoped for sympathy, but in vain. I found no one to console me".

2b. *Dukachem konddo.* Reference to the *Salve Regina ... in hac lachrymarum valle,* "in this valley of tears" - which phrase is translated as "pool of tears/pool of misery" by Father Thomas Stephens (*duqhachea conddantu*).

4d. *Vor mak' tuj' rajantum.* Reminiscent of the prayer of the Good Thief on the Cross: "Lord, remember me when you come into your kingdom" (*Luke* 23: 42).

Villap 19. LUSITANO RODRIGUES (+1943)
Soglem mujem vido chintunum Vellu muzo karhtam rorhunum

TESTIMONY TO AUTHORSHIP. The author's compilation, *Cantos do povo.* 1, p. 4, where he says: "Composto por L. Rodrigues".

SOURCE OF SCORE. *Op. cit., loc. cit.*

SOURCE OF TEXT. Ibid.

VARIANTS. The text of the mando is Barhdexified by the Saxtti author who, had he sung the mando himself, would have used unmodified Saxtti throughout. In Luzitano's time most Goan Christians had come to believe that Barhdexi was the standard dialect of Konkani. Here the following Barhdexi forms have been replaced by their Saxtti equivalents: *vidu* (1a) by *vido* ; *konnum* (1c) by *konnom* ; *buzvonnu* (1d) by *buzvonnom* ; and *mortots* (3c) by *mortrich.*

MUSICAL FORM. Ternary.

LITERARY FORM. Monologue mando.

Villap 20. UTÍLCIA REBELO (1886/87-1960)
Kity'm kon-n sanddun gel' re maka

TESTIMONY TO AUTHORSHIP. Authoress herself, in 1954 and 1959; Semeão and Plácido Costa.

DATE. 1933, a year after the death of the authoress's husband, as she herself informed us.

SOURCE OF SCORE. André Costa and Plácido Costa.

SOURCE OF TEXT. Authoress, 10 June 1959.

DEDICATION. To authoress's husband, who died on 15 October 1932, and to her mother, who died on 21 December 1931.

ANECDOTES IN THE HISTORY OF THE SONG. We first met Utílcia Rebelo in 1954. She was lying ill on her bed in one of the small rooms of her little house, which was all that remained of the family's once large residence. The sunshine came in through the only window in the room to her right, lighting its rough woodwork, the ramshackle bed covered with old rags, the blankets wrapped round her, picking out the expressive lines of her old aristocratic head. Aires Menezes, the photographer took a picture of her, the only known (and now lost) likeness of the authoress. From that bed and its surroundings, Utílcia took us back to the great days of the Mando, which she had witnessed. She sang us many fine old songs, as well as her own compositions, including the present mando.

MUSICAL FORM. Ternary.

LITERARY FORM. Monologue mando.

ALLUSIONS. 1e. *Sorgary Deva' tsoicha' maka.* The only reference in the mandos to the Beatific Vision that we know of.

APPENDICES

Appendix 1

Rules of Saxtti Elision

The language of the Mando is Bambonn Saxtti, the dialect spoken by the Brahmins of Saxtty/Salcete, particularly in the villages of Lotlli, Kurhtori, Rai, Morhgoum and Bannali. Saxtti, in all its caste variations (which are leveling off in the 21st century), is distinguished from other Konkani dialects by its extensive use of elision - the omission of vowels, consonants or syllables in pronunciation. Konkani is an inflectional language: it modifies the form of its words by adding affixes or by changing the shape of a base to express different grammatical relations. In a Saxtti sentence, all the words can be elided, with the following exceptions:

1. The last word in the sentence. *Aim' kolls' fol-llo*, or *Kolls' fol-ll' anvem* (*Anvem kollso fol-llo/Kollso fol-llo anvem.* "I have broken the water jar").
2. Words ending in nasals. *Tuge' maink igojjê' gelô' dekylô' anvem* (*Tugele maink igorjjek geloli dekyloli anvem.* "I saw your mother go to church").
3. Most words ending in consonants, nominative case. *Mujan tuk' sang' nuzo. (Mujan tuka sangunk nuzo.* "I can't tell you"). *Dukor mely'm munn anim sunny'm jivy'm as' munn fobor aikily' anvem* (*Dukor melem munn anim sunnem jivem asa munn fobor aikilea anvem.* "I have heard the news that the pig is dead and that the dog is alive").
4. Words ending in the semivowel *y*. *Maram' Pedr' sangta' apnnangê' barhkany mel-llö' munn.* (*Marantso Pedru sangtulo apnnangeli barhkany mel-lloli munn.* "Pedru the mhar was saying that he had met his landlady").

In elision, words follow the rules indicatēd below:

VOWELS: *a*, *o*, *u* are dropped; *e*, *i*, are substituted by the semivowel *y*.

a	*zala > zal'*
e, ea, eo	*zale, zalea, zaleo > zaly'*
i	*zali > zaly'*
o	*zalo > zal'*
u	*durhu > durh' (duddu, money)*

SYLLABLES WITH NASALS. Nasals retained; vowels eliminated as per rules

am	*zalam > zal'm*
em	*zalem > zaly'm*
im	*zalim > zaly'm*
om	*zalom > zal'm*
um	*cherhum > cherh'm*

CONSONANTS

Dative: *-ak,-ek, -ank*	*diullak > diulla' ; marvank > marvam'*
Locative: *-ant, -int*	*atant > atam' ; kailint > kailim'*
Infinitive: *-unk, -chak*	*marunk > marum' ; zauchak > zaucha'*

AFFIXES

Genitive: *tso-chi-chem*	*bottatso, bottachi, bottachem > bottats', bottach', bottach'm* or just *botta'*
Genitive: *lo-li-lem*	*bottalo, bottali, bottalem > bottal', bottaly', bottaly'm* or just *botta'*
Past indicative: *lom-lim-lem*	*ailolom, ailolim, ailolem > ailol'm, ailôly'm, ailòly'm,* or *ailom', ailôm', ailòly'm*
Future subjunctive in *-ry*	*zaleary > zalea'*
Post-positions in *-ry*	*barabory > barabô' bar'bô'; amgery > amgê'; bitory > bito'; mukary > muka'*
Post-positions in *-rhe*	*takorhe > takorhy' > tako'*

INTERNAL ELISION

barabory > bar'bô'	*Cherh' gorvam' bar'bô' gela (cherho gorvanche barabori gela,* "the boy has gone with the cattle")

Appendix 2

Lives of the Three Major Composers: Arnaldo, Gizelino, and Torquato

Arnaldo de Menezes (1863-1917)

In the following essay Arnaldo's life is described on the basis of what his friends told us about him.

The home of the Arnaldo's immediate ancestors was the Xennoibag (Sinaibaga) ward of Kurhtori/Curtorim on the banks of the Mai Tollem, the large monsoon lake that a low ridge of hills separates from the river Zuari. His parents were Aleixo Santana do Espírito Santo Menezes, a well-to-do landowner, and Ana Teodosia Ubaldina Luís. Living with them was his paternal uncle, locally known as Mone Nistady (Manuel Natividade?).

Facing the lake, to the east of it, at Vonvottem/Anvottem, is the chapel of Nossa Senhora do Carmo (1783); a road runs along it to the north, to Morhgoum/Margão. Aleixo moved from his ancestral home to a place along this road, to the north of the chapel, probably before Arnaldo was born. He had four children, two boys (Amâncio, the eldest, and later a priest, and our Arnaldo, the youngest of the children), and two girls (Aldosinha and Rutilante). Arnaldo was born on 16 July 1863 - the eve of the feast of the patron saint of the Kurhtori church, Santo Aleixo (or St. Alex), and on the feast day of Our Lady of Carmel, patroness of the chapel. These events were incorporated in his name - Arnaldo Cesisnando do Carmo Vespera de Santo Aleixo de Menezes.

Arnaldo received his elementary training at the parish school, where he was also taught Latin, the catechism, the Bible story and music - which included training in the violin and in plainsong (*cantochão*). As was the custom in those days, he later went to study at the Seminário de Rachol/Raitur, it is not clear for how long, probably three years. His violin teacher is reported to have been a well-qualified musician, probably a priest, who was greatly impressed by his pupil's talent. The young Arnaldo also studied under mestre Rodolfo Teles, one of the many musical virtuosos that blossomed at Kurhtori at the turn of the 19th century. (Teles also taught other musicians, like the doctor Aleixo António Costa, the priest Floriano Rodrigues, Diogo Vaz and mestre Rosário Moniz). Rodolfo was murdered (no one knows why) in 1900. He was staggering by a house, drunk, when he was invited inside, and plied with more drink. When he was completely intoxicated, the murderers put an iron band round his head, and tightened it with a screw till his skull cracked. They then threw the corpse into an old well.

Arnaldo became proficient in the violin and the double bass, and was an excellent player of the *gumott,* a pot-shaped ceramic drum covered on one side with taut lizard skin. Once on a feast of St. John the Baptist (*Son-Joaum*), when Goan boys and men enjoy themselves by jumping into the rain-filled wells, Arnaldo was walking along a steep wet road on the hill to the west of the chapel: he slipped, fell and injured his right arm. Ever afterwards he is said to have used his left arm (kept in a still position) in playing the violin. He was familiar with a lot of classical music: at his death his relatives (who possessed none of his knowledge and skill) burnt twenty printed scores.

He was thus well equipped to be a composer of mandos, mostly inspired by love of women. Many anecdotes were told about his passion for them, how they had sometimes to jump over walls to avoid his advances. Even small girls felt unease at his approach; one of them, later a grown woman, recalled how she approached him with a piece of dry, cow-dung cake (*xenni*), to light his country cigar (*virhi*) with. The late Dr. Semeão Costa, one of his closest friends, recounts how Arnaldo, with some of his friends, saw some women, dressed in *voly,* walking in front of them. Sensing the approach of the men, the women, as custom demanded, drew the flap of hood of their *voly* closer, to conceal their faces. Queried Arnaldo, "Would you like to see the women's faces?" (*Tumy'm bailam' tonddam' tsoitlei-i?*). "Then come with me!" At this they quickened their pace till they were well in front of the women. Suddenly the men turned and faced the women, who had in the meantime slid the *voly* flaps back when the men had overtaken them, and were too stunned to draw them closer again.

Arnaldo was enamored of many women, and hoped to marry them, but they mostly rejected him. The first woman he wooed seems to have been one Luisa Pereira; she married a man nicknamed "Ranno"; it was Arnaldo who accompanied her to her wedding. He later fell in love with a future Mrs. Xavier, and still later, a future Mrs. Costa. He was not a good loser when ousted, as the mando on Mrs. Xavier - *Anvem sangilolem tuka Dusman zaunum dakoinaka* - which casts malicious aspersions on her birth, shows.

A woman whom he developed a passion for was one Maria Angélica (or *Maryanjol*), as she was popularly known, a woman who later acquired a notorious reputation. He went to court her on a moonlit night. As he approached her house, he caught a glimpse of her standing at the entrance to her porch, when mother came rushing and slammed the door in the ardent lover's face. On the spur of the moment, Arnaldo improvised a mando, which begins:

Tsondrimancha uzvarhanum
Mannyka dekily'm mum go tuka
Surya porim porzollito
Mannyka tujem sarkem dislem maka

This skill in improvisation did not open Maryanjol's door, but it served him at weddings, soirées and other social functions.

Being rejected so often caused Arnaldo much unhappiness, and many of his finest mandos are saturated with his personal grief. Alternation between romantic infatuation and bleak despondency seems to have made up a major part of his life. The woman who caused him the greatest suffering appears to have been one Teodósia (or Teodosinha, to her friends). For her he composed one of his most tender mandos:

Anju munnum tum sorgintso
Uzvarh zala noketrantso
Amtso mogu ekttaim kortso
Cazrats' sacramentu geutso

Nuzo, nuzo re mujan
Tuje vinnem sonsar tanddum' nuzo

Utílcia Rebelo, herself a mando composer and sister to the composer Gizelino, once saw them sitting gaily by the well of Teodosinha's house.

But as time passed, these visits became less and less frequent. (Teodosinha was engaged to someone else; they were unwilling to marry her to Arnaldo, who was 38 while she was 19.) He took to writing letters to her, which were never answered. He then borrowed a book from her house, *Moço instruído,* and soon made as though he had finished reading it, with a letter hidden between its leaves. There was no reply. At another time he sent the letters through a friend, with no better results.

Arnaldo expressed his frustration at this rejection in two rude mandos, filled with innuendos, describing the goings-on in the bride's house in preparation for the wedding, one of which was the prospective bridegroom, Fidelino Costa, running away with the bride's wedding necklace, the work of six goldsmiths. These mandos are: *Kurhtream' konnom re foboro* and *Copela' sokol amgely'm goro Dogaincheim gorhit zaloly'm oro*. Some say that Arnaldo improvised the latter as he was passing by the house at night. The marriage took place on 12 February 1901. (Teodosinha's son, Plácido Costa, is one of the greatest informants on the mando and on several other types of Konkani Song.)

Finally, a lovely lady agreed to be his wife, Ezilda Barreto. She was considerably younger than him, and she was still alive in the 1960s. The inroads of old age had not obliterated her beauty, described by some of her companions as queenly. They had no children, which worried Arnaldo greatly; so they adopted a boy named Cipriano, who became his foster-father's heir.

But Arnaldo never lost his affection for Teodosinha; he never stopped teasing her about her marriage to Fidelino. Once when the two couples had gone to the seaside resort at Mazod-ddem/ Majorda, Arnaldo sang one of the mandos, which he had composed to ridicule Teodosinha's wedding, with the allusion to the necklace in the very first verse:

Kurhtream' konnom re fobŏro
Baravery as' munttai cazaro
Maim-ti kori tum rozaro
Tsoiche furhem kontteachem bangaro

Teodosinha replied with a *dulpod,* hinting (not without malice) at Arnaldo's childlessness:

Gou-bailam dogaim vanzurhim saiba
Burgem naim gor-dera
Lokaly'm burgem an-nn poxilam
"Papa" *munnum' maka*

Arnaldo was very fond of his wife, and believed that forbearance made for a good marriage. As he said in the last verse of his own wedding mando, *Zaito tempu anvem balanddilo*:

Vellu aileary amcheri dukantso
Sonsar somzunum tanddumtso
Dogainch'm kalliz kornum eko
Diso karhche amy'm daduso

In 1915 Arnaldo - aware as few others with what love and marriage had to offer - composed a model wedding mando, *Chintinastonn' ekvottu zalo Sorgu maka dislo.* This and variations of it have been sung time and time again.

Besides love, Arnaldo was aware of that other human emotion, envy, from which he himself was not wholly free. In one of his most perceptive mandos, he thus characterizes this plague of Goan life, which he saw embodied in the doings of his neighbor Idalfo Menezes:

Oromb nuim re amcha Gointso
Dusrea feliz mum re tsoutso
O xirap nuim konnantso
Gunnum y amcha zalolea terratso

Sonsrach' funnom kol-lli re maka
Suko naka

Toward the end of his life, something tragic happened which gave him the opportunity for composing his masterpiece, "The Adolfinian Trilogy". A friend from Morhgoum/Margão, Adolfinho Costa (1864-1914) by name, was madly in love with one Adelina, also a Costa, and perhaps a near relative. Arnaldo, shopping in the Mercado Novo (New Market) in that town, happened to see him in the street, lonely and unhappy, continually letting out loud sighs (*Ai! Ai!*). When asked why, Adolfinho told his friend that Adelina was to be married to another man (Vicente Caetano Barbosa by name). Arnaldo decided that the best he could do was to compose a mando by which Adolfinho could publicly declaim his misfortune. (In that mando he would incorporate the *Ai! Ai!* Of the lover's sighs.)

The wedding morning, of 19 April 1901, was rainy and wet. As Adelina was dressing for the wedding, Adolfinho was on his knees in the murk outside begging her to change her mind while there was still time. He then followed her to the church (of the Holy Spirit, Espírito Santo). Weddings in those days were celebrated at the main portal of the church, and not before the altar, as they are nowadays. Before the assembled wedding guests, the unhappy lover lay down at the center of the raised platform before the church portal, stretching out his arms in the form of a cross, appearing as though intoxicated by his own agony. In that posture he launched his last desperate appeal to his adored Adelina:

Tuzo mogu axlol' munnum
Morhgounts' borla sogloch gaum-um
Kallzach' gutto tuje mujery dovornum
Y Atam morum' paulam y aum-um

Ai! Ai! Ontoskornanche gave re muje
Ai! Ai! Konnanko dakoiche!

But the marriage ceremony went on regardless. Adolfinho, from now a broken man, tried to drown his misery in drink. Neglected by his relatives, he died in the Hospício of his native town, three years before his friend Arnaldo.

But *Tuzo mogu* was not the only mando that Arnaldo composed for Adolfinho. Soon afterwards, he produced the *Motim' sopnnantum naxlolem*, which passers-by used to see the rejected lover sing from the veranda of his house, tears streaming down his cheeks. Arnaldo's wife Ezilda, in 1954, related how she and her husband were on their way to Morhgoum one morning in their horse-drawn carriage, when they sighted Adolfinho, who was walking towards them, motioning them to stop. He wanted a mando composed, and insisted on accompanying Arnaldo back to the latter's house in Kurhtori. Ezilda recalled how she heard both men discussing in the hall, with Arnaldo singing (or composing) a mando, and Adolfinho listening and suggesting changes. This mando was doubtless the *Motim' sopnnantum naxlolem*.

Before Adolfinho's tragedy, Arnaldo had composed a mando on his own sad predicament (he was suffering from some sexually transmitted disease, syphilis?). Adolfinho adopted this mando – the *Chintun furhar Deva muzo* - and sang it as though it had been especially composed for him. There are some who still believe that it was, and others relate that Adolfinho claimed that it was his own composition (he was no composer). However, the three mandos fit together so well, and their succession is such a convincing expression of change of mood and emotion – from desperate appeal to black hopelessness – that they deserve a title expressive of this unity, such as "The Adolfinian Trilogy".

Arnaldo's life was not all sadness, however. He had a band of companions who, like himself loved practical jokes. One of these companions was Ligório Costa (1840-1917), known as *Penkaum Ligóry*, apparently the oldest dateable mando composer of Kurhtori. Another was Azavedo Diniz (1860-1907), who has some fine dulpods and at least one mando to his credit; he was himself a practical joker. People relate how, on a day in Holy Week, Azavedo put on a cassock and sat in the confessional. An elderly lady entered the confessional and poured all her sins in the phony priest's ears. When she had finished, he stepped out of the confessional muttering, "You poor thing " (*bong'm tujem*)! There are people who believe that the perpetrator of this blasphemous joke was Arnaldo himself.

Before speaking of the acts of mischief that are Arnaldo's beyond a doubt, mention must be made of Arnaldo's love of a good meal. A woman named Aninha Rangel, born in the 1880s and alive in 1960, relates how she received a call from the *regidor* of Kurhtori and Arnaldo at her home at Maina, a ward of the same village. She was then a young mother, and there was no one else at home but her little son.

Arnaldo, always impudent, invited himself to a meal with the words, "Come, sit at the table, and let's have lunch" (*Yo go, mezache' bois go, jeunnanko*).

Aninha, who did not want to serve Arnaldo a meal, replied, "I'll eat in the kitchen" (*Aum cujnantum jeutam*).

"Then you must have something special in the kitchen!" (*Cujnam' kitem punn as' zatolem*) remarked Arnaldo. (Aninha had in fact prepared a dish of pork, and was not keen on sharing it with the composer.) Arnaldo was also very fond of liquor, but for the sake of a woman that he loved, and for whom he wrote *Noketrancha porzoll' porim* (*Utrike* 26), he kept away from it for two full years.

To return to the pranks of Arnaldo and friends. A vicar was preaching on the immorality of the Carnival, and while he was doing so, these young men slunk out of church and armed themselves with earthenware pots (*kollxe*), which they filled with colored water. As the unsuspecting congregation was leaving the church, they were doused with that tinted liquid. At another carnival the youths wore dhotis (*puddvim*), and shouldering a stretcher with a straw figure representing a corpse, took it to a field behind the Nossa Senhora do Carmo chapel, and set it on fire amid songs and loud cries: they were parodying the Hindu ceremony of cremation. Some say that instead of straw figure, they had the image of a goddess belonging to the village goldsmith Ori (Hari). The lads also composed a folk style play, of a type that is usually staged at Carnivals, a true *fell*.

At a festival of Gonnespoti (Ganpati, the elephant god) they played a practical joke on the poor goldsmith. In this festival, the image of the god is worshiped in Hindu houses for some days, and then immersed in a sea, river or well. On the day of the immersion, one of the company, armed with rope, ladder and net, hid himself in the well where the image was to be thrown. Caught in the net, the image was recovered, at night, and left on Ori's doorstep - where the horrified goldsmith found it the next day. Arnaldo composed new verses to an old *deknni* tune (sung in the days when the railway was being built in Goa, 1881-1886), beginning with the words, *Gonnespoti raya Taka salamm y amim korya*. One of the verses clearly refers to the above event:

Allvantulean gelolo Gonnes
Fuim paulo to pollya
Bettek lagun pollun gela
Orile baintum sodya

To these impish youths, nothing appears to have been sacred.

An unfortunate Goan institution was that of the *beatinny*, or devout spinster. For a variety of reasons, economic (inability to pay dowries) and social (need for someone to care for aged parents), many women were compelled to be single. These women had little to occupy themselves with except their devotions and gossip. Arnaldo wrote scathing mandos on them, one of which begins with the words, *Amchem odruxtt kituly'm vorho Sangum' yenam mak' utoro*, of which verse 5 reads:

Sarkem dakoitai anjachem
Formonn geunum deutsarachem
Farsanch'm ulonny'm mum re tanchem
Tsoleanch' toklê' laicha' pixem

Vitsva' baxen gunnum tantso
Sonsar sogloch uportun portuntso

A preacher actually made a *beatinny* mando (the one quoted?) the text of one of his sermons, and publicly called a blessing on the composer for writing it. While the sermon was going on, all were staring at Arnaldo, who was embarrassed and jubilant.

Other occasions where Arnaldo shone were weddings. There he could exercise his uncommon talent for singing and dancing and improvisation. Two rooms were set aside for receptions, the card room and the ballroom. There were more card players than dancers then, and people in the 1960s still remembered how the players dropped their cards and made a dash for the ballroom when, accompanied by the thump on the *gumott*, the sound of Arnaldo's singing fell on their ears.

In such functions, Arnaldo sang the old songs and those he himself had composed; but he also modified the old ones, and adapted them to the situations at hand. Some types of songs allowed for improvisation, like wedding songs. One variety of such songs is sung when people hand in their presents, along with their blessing, in the presence of the bride and the groom. The songs are generally short, and sometimes mildly provocative descriptions of each person as each takes his turn.

Arnaldo always made sure that he got right the facts relevant to the person to be described, before the singing started. The story is told of a man who was present at one such function, whose passion for a girl ("Leonor") had been exciting comment. He had left the Seminary and had gone to the *Liceu* to study, but of late had been spending much time with the girl in question. Going up to the student, Arnaldo placed a book (symbol of studentship) into his hands, and returning to his seat, started to improvise on a *dulpod* that begins:

Estud sanddun bountam munn
Tuka sangilolem konnem
Anim carto y anvem kal-llam go Leonor
Juridic xikuch' furhem

Arnaldo had the uncanny gift of finding the right *dulpod for* the right person. The following is one such *dulpod* that referred to a plump woman present in the hall:

Tondd tsoileary disot katllê' ollem
Bendd tsoileary disot' tonnam' kurhem
Konnem tujery galy'm go
Tem mannxechem follem

No one was free from his barbs, even the absent, or yet even the dead. An exceptionally skinny man, nicknamed *Barkelo* (Mr. Skinny) had recently died. This was Arnaldo's chance to parody a popular *deknni*, which runs as follows:

Bottu melo, botta' gobor zalo
Bottiny meli, botnnim' mati zali

Arnaldo changed the first line into *Barkel' melo, barkelea' gobor zalo.* It is not known what he did with the second line.

Singing, dancing and improvising sometimes exhausted our composer, and he is once known to have fainted at the wedding of one João Caetano at Kurhtori. He was fed with little spoonfuls of risotto (*arroz*) to help him get his strength back. He would also get quite drunk, as he did when attending a wedding at Morhgoum as a young man. After a furious quarrel with somebody, he set out on his trek back home. It was a dark night; the sky was overcast with clouds. But his mind was not completely fogged. He inched his way up the black road, and when there was a flash of lightning, he ran ahead swiftly to cover as much ground while the light of the flash lasted.

He once sang with his friend Paulo Milagres Silva of Lotlli (author of the sublime *Eko vorso bolanddilem*) in the presence of António Sérgio, Governor of Goa from 1877 to 1878. Amâncio Gracias says that both Paulo and Arnaldo composed the score of the mando that was sung on that occasion. An even more memorable event was the Exposition of the body of St. Francis Xavier in Velha Goa in 1900. Among the pilgrims were Arnaldo (from Kurhtori) and Torquato de Figueiredo (of Lotlli). Travel from these villages to the old metropolis in those days was on foot, by ox- and horse-carriages, launch, or fishermen's sailing boats (*orhim*). Each of these boats could take about thirty, and this was the mode of conveyance that our two pilgrims adopted.

Each village had a day fixed for the kissing of the saint's feet. Our two composers, belonging as they did to different villages, may have arrived separately, but they left the old city at 5 on the same evening, stopping at the island of Kumbarzuem (Combarjua) for the night. Here they lit fires, and settled down to a meal of rice and curried fish. Dinner over, the music session began, in the presence of the two greatest luminaries of Goan Song. The lordly mandos of Arnaldo and Torquato were followed by cascading dulpods, and periods of melodic solemnity and gloom were rounded off by an orgy of spasmodic and scintillating tunes - until it was nearly dawn, and time to set out for home.

For some reason, the relationship of the two men, cordial at the start, seems to have cooled off as their trip was nearing its end. The pilgrims from Lotlli got off at Raitur, and those for Kurhtori kept on. It is not certain whether they ever met afterwards.

We know how unsparing Arnaldo could be in the use of strong language when he disliked something. He was constantly sniping at people he thought were "poisonous" (*vikar;* a favorite phrase with him was *To vikar mum re!*). When once Gizelino's mother asked why he wrote such mean-spirited mandos (*arê, ox'm kot-tai-i rê?*), he is said to have replied that it was due to his anger (*rag*) and childishness (*burgyponn).* These mandos made him unpopular, and many people believe that his childlessness was due to the curses laid upon him by those whom he had vilified.

Also living in Vonvottem, nearer the chapel than Arnaldo, was his less dazzling rival, Gizelino Rebelo (1875-1932), the second of our Big Three. Unlike his older contemporary, he was a self-made musician, more introvert and perhaps more sensitive to suffering. Their ideas and style were similar. In the last years of his life, Arnaldo used to claim authorship of the mando, *Kosleim dizgras mum re mujem At'm y anvy'm konnanko sanguchem,* which is probably more Gizelino's than his. Arnaldo's wife, who also believed that the author was her husband, related how he used to sing it to her, keeping the time of the song with gentle taps on her head. Two of Gizelino's mandos, *Chintun caba' korum' nuzo Mirhmirhy' bogtai te kallyzako* and *Kosleim vido mum re y amchem Chintleary moronn fursavelem,* have often been mistaken for Arnaldo's. Gizelino, for his part, used to say that one of Arnaldo's mandos, *Sintment varoily' e sonsrako Tsounuz' duk ek tuj' dolleanko,* that it was so near to his heart, and so intimately expressive of his own inner feelings, that he would have liked it to have been his own. However, the two composers do not seem to have become close friends, and the older man used to say rude things about his younger rival, calling him

Sutkar, in allusion to a mistress of Gizelino's at Kon-jem/Corjem, though it is hard to see what the word means. Gizelino is also reported to have been equally uncomplimentary about his older rival, but no information is available about what exactly he said.

Later in life Arnaldo began to grow somewhat bald, and took to wearing a monocle. He never quite lost his attractiveness. In addition, he was fair skinned ("like a *paklo*"), of a pinker skin color than is usual in Goa.

The fatal venereal disease he had contracted in his hot youth was the reason for his untimely death, though the official cause was *angina pectoris*. He died on the night of 7-8 December at about midnight or one in the morning. One of these days was a first Friday, and the 8th was of course the feast of the Immaculate Conception. He received the last sacraments, and it appears that he was in full possession of his senses till the very end. His wife was at his side, and to her he sang the last verse of their wedding song. On their wedding day he had, in the 4th verse of his marriage mando (quoted earlier) *looked forward* to overcoming any troubles that they might have to face. Now he *looked back* to their happy life together, how they had faced those troubles and had overcome:

Vellu eunum mujery dukantso
Sonsar somzunum ***tanddilo***
Dogainch'm kalliz kornum eko
Diso ***kal-lle*** *amy'm daduso*

Arnaldo's mortal remains repose in the village cemetery of Kurhtori, on the inner wall to the right of the entrance.

Gizelino Rebelo (1875-1931)

Gizelino's father, from Vernnem, and his mother, from Kurhtori, were married on 7 February 1871. They had six children, three boys and three girls. The eldest was Belisário (1871-1942); the second, our composer Gizelino; the third, Eurinda (1878-1953); the fourth, Genserico (1882-1960); and the fifth, Utílcia (1886/7-1960), the last important Mando composer. We have no information about the sixth child.

Gizelino was born on 30 January 1875 at his mother's house at Kurhtori. His full name was José Gizelino de Jesus Teófilo Tomás do

Rosário Aleixo Eufemiano dos Milagres e Piedade Rebelo. We do not know the exact date of his father's death, but it was sometime after 1886. The mother, however, outlived her son and died on 21 December 1931. Gizelino's early years were spent in the company of his siblings at Vernnem, at the house of their Aunt Amélia, a hard woman who would ill-treat them and give them very little to eat (*dony douly' bo' xit*, "two ladlefuls of rice"). Amelia had an orchard of guava trees; she would prepare guava cheese and send it to her sister's, but the children were allowed to touch neither the cheese nor the fruit. The woman's cruelty left its mark on the boy's sensitive mind.

The house in which Gizelino grew up to young manhood was a large one, with a number of servants. Among them was a Teresa, whom Gizelino was fond of; as was his younger brother Genserico. So jealous did he grow of Teresa's attention to Gizelino, that he tried to shoot the girl. A quarrel ensued, and the younger brother appears to have been soundly thrashed. On her part, the girl was not very tactful about Gizelino's fondness for her, and babbled about her love affair with her young master; she did so once in the presence of the sisters Eurinda and Utílcia. Brought up as they had been along strict aristocratic lines, the girls felt that they had to show a mere maid her place. One of them took a bit of dried cow-dung cake (*xenny*), which was burning at one end, and struck Teresa on the mouth with it, telling her that she could open what she liked, so long as she kept her mouth shut (*kitem orh kory, tondd ol-lly'm kon-naka*). So, quite early in life, Gizelino got involved in love, as he was to do afterwards, though not as often as Arnaldo.

Aunt Amélia now made her presence felt again. As her husband was probably impotent, she took a lover, José, the son of her sister-in-law. The people who knew her then had no doubt that she had killed his two children, the first probably by poisoning and the second by throwing it into a well. She was violently against her husband's trying to get Gizelino married, as other young women in the family might either distract José or curtail Amélia's privacy with him, so she threatened to leave the house by the back door the moment Gizelino would bring his bride in through the front door.

But Gizelino did not brood over his unhappy life, at least not always. He was a naturally exuberant man, fond of dancing and singing, and of giving people a fright. He taught his sister Utílcia funny songs, took her to dances and showed her the steps of the

Contredanse, the Lancers, and of course the Mando. She was afraid of water, and he once scared her by taking her to the large Mai Tollem lake and making as if he would drown her in it.

By this time, he had imbibed all the education he was ever to have, the *estudos elementar* and *complementar*, and some Latin and English. He appears to have had little formal training in music, and was mostly a self-made musician, familiar with the works of trained composers (personally known to him), and of the compositions of church music.

Gizelino's love life did not end with his affair with Teresa. When about 32 he appears to have become seriously enamored of a Julieta Barreto, for whom he wrote one of his mandos, the *Inocenti mujem vido Surya pax'm nitollo nirmollo*. Julieta may or may not have liked Gizelino, but she married another man, a school-teacher. At another time, he lost his heart to another woman, Clara Menezes, who also refused to marry him. The pain of her rejection led him to compose one of the best known and loved of the mandos, the *Surya noketranche porim porzolleta* (*Utrike* 32). There was another woman in his life, but her nickname, "Bichinha," is all we know about her.

Later, our unhappy composer was to fall in love again, this time to a married woman, Nascimenta Cruz, one of his tenants in the ward of Kon'jem/Corgem. For her he wrote *Nitoll nirmoll sarkem anjachem*. He used to see her so often that people began to suspect that they were having an affair. Gizelino seems to have been highly sexed; he is known to have kept a Hindu mistress. And however much he may himself have wanted to marry, he was not sympathetic to his own sister's, Utílcia's, desire to do so - and she was the only one of the Rebelos who ever wedded - for it meant that some of the family wealth would leave the house as dowry, something that caused a typical Brahmin landed proprietor (like Gizelino) great distress. But Utílcia would not listen; she asked for and got a dowry of Rs. 12,000. Gizelino stayed a whole day without food and went to bed fasting.

He continued to pay visits to Nascimenta, however. She had as neighbors two elderly spinsters, *beatinnys*, known as Emad and Efu, daughters of a Paixão Rebelo (or "Paixaum Tiu"). Annoyed by their (far from baseless) gossip, he wrote a corrosive mando lampooning all *beatinnys*, the *Zaitea tsorha re tempanom*, supposed by some to be the first of the *beatinny* mandos.

Worse things could happen at Kurhtori than the mere prying

of spinsters, tragedies of love more terrible than just scandal. In 1922, when our composer was 47, Mário Rodrigues, a youth of 21, killed himself. He was in love with a girl of the Menezes family (was it Clara herself again?), who does not seem to have loved Mário at all. There was to be a dance party in a large mansion in the village; she was to be there, and Mário too, but he had by now begun to despair of the girl's love. Calling on the village doctor, Aleixo António Costa (1874-1936, himself a composer of mandos), he told him that he had a dog that he wanted to destroy, and inquired how much poison was needed to kill it. Mário made the unsuspecting doctor give him a greater dose than was needed to finish off any animal of the species. That evening, the girl did not appear to be keen to dance with him; she was not on dance floor, but in a gallery above it. Mário got himself a glass of wine from the bar, and put the poison in it for all to see. Then raising the glass to her in a dramatic gesture, to signify that he was drinking to her health, he swallowed the wine in a gulp and raced out of the house excitedly, down the path that leads from the mansion to the main road, and then turned to the right, where the road winds to the Kurhtori church and to Mário's house. He ran a few yards and fell. There was an outcry, and when the members of his family came to try and save his life, the young man was found to be barely breathing. He died in the cart (or horse carriage) that was taking him home. A cross marks the site where he fell.

This tragedy deeply moved Gizelino. Opposite his house was a shop owned by his friend *Dall* Marian (the composer Mariano Costa, 1898-1931), one of the best mando singers in the village. There he wrote the mando that commemorates Mário's death - *Zaite vorsanch' muje baie*. Gizelino changed the sex of the suicide so as not to get in trouble with the family of the Menezes girl. In the same shop, and about the same time, Gizelino is said to have composed his *Surya noketranche porim porzolleta.*

Though darkened by tragedy, Gizelino's life was not unmitigatedly sad, but was lightened by routine and fun. He was a landowner, and the work of supervising his tenants took a large part of his time. He loved dancing (as we noted), fishing, and grafting, as well as hunting. He danced at weddings and greatly enjoyed himself when anything incongruous occurred - as when the crackers went off before the right moment at the wedding of an Esmeraldinha, for which occasion he wrote the *Surya sontosan udelo*

(*Ekvott* 10). Gizelino was also fond of dulpods and Kunnbi songs. He seems to have enjoyed fishing, and this sometimes caused other people trouble. Once he could hardly tear himself away from the riverside, and so arrived home very late. His mother was worried. Before he got back, however, a friend, Axu Azevedo (for whose wedding he wrote the *Diso ekleponnantule*, *Ekvott* 6) entered the house in the dark and the mother (not being able to make out who it was and thinking it was Gizelino) beat him with her slipper, Axu calling out, "Why are you hitting me?" (*Mak' mat-ta re, mak' mat-ta re?*). Gizelino was fond of fish and liked a lot of it with his rice. When, after his successful fishing trips, he had a good meal, he would say, "Could anyone have eaten as well as me today in Vonvottem" (*Muj' baxen aj konnom Anvotteam' joul' zaito*)? As for *pez*, the rice-gruel beloved of Goans, he felt that it was not tasty enough if there were not a heap of fish and crab meat to go along with it.

He also liked chicken. Gizelino and brother Genserico, who used to look after their estates at Vernnem, often came to Kurhtori to visit their mother. On such occasions, she would give them the best part of the chicken (which, otherwise, was Utílcia's usual portion). Then Utílcia would sulk, and refuse to eat her rice with anything but pickles (*solantum' ambarhe*). Her grandmother once noticed this, and cooked Utílcia a whole chicken when her brothers had left.

His hunting provided him with tasty meat, but he was not above stealing what other hunters had bagged. One morning, when he was brushing his teeth, a bird shot by some hunters fell near to where he was. He picked it up and hid it under a pile of dry leaves. When the hunters came along and inquired whether he had seen it, he said that he had not, and had the bird cooked after they had gone. Hunting exposed him to many dangers in Goa's dense jungles. On one expedition he came across a tigress (or she-leopard) and her two cubs, but lived to tell the tale.

Gizelino was fond of jokes, especially at others' expense. Once when a firecracker went off, he is said to have made an obscene comment, whose drift we cannot recall. At another time, he was sent to see someone whom he found asleep. When he got back he imitated the sleeper's bewilderment when awakened (*Bilom, usol-llom, bairy pol-llom*, "I was scared, I jumped, I fell out!"). Sometimes he amused himself by fomenting quarrels, as in the case of an old woman and a younger lady relative, by telling the older person that the younger one had sold two of her rose apple (*jambul*) trees. Not every kind of entertainment found favor with him, however, and he was often seen to walk out of the room where men played cards.

Being an active landlord, he had a practical mind, knowing both how to do things and to get things done. He once spotted how one Lambusquinho, a wily carpenter of Makzon/Macasana, widened doors that were a trifle narrow by soaking them in water and beating them. At another time he relieved a woman's acute stomach-ache, which she had developed by eating too many guavas, by giving her a cucumber. She was pregnant and was to give birth to *Xeto* Rosário, born in 1913, a song-writer of sorts, and alive in the 1970s.

Our composer never seems to have left Goa, though his hunting may have taken him over much of its area. He is known to have visited Bannali/Benaulim, Morhgoum, Makzon, Dramapur and Nagvem/Nagoa, and perhaps also Ponnji and Lotlli. He once went to Morhgoum to bathe at a well known spring, Tollsam' zory, and, shocked at seeing men and women bathing there together, returned and gave vent to his indignation in the dulpod *E te Tollsam' zori' barik gogo*. He was also conscious of the political events that impacted Goa, like the election of a popular governor, Mariano Martins (in office between 1925 and 1926), an event which he commemorated in his mando *Aji sontos re Indieko*.

Most of the mandos, which Gizelino composed, were, however, marriage songs, and many people would request him to write a mando for their wedding. One such man was a tailor, Pedro Sequeira e Melo, an orphan who had been brought up by a landlord, also a Melo, of Kurhtori. The latter did not want his charge to marry; and when he did, disinherited him. On another occasion, a man wanted Gizelino to compose a mando for him, and when our musician asked the man what he wanted said in the song, the reply was, "there is a feeling of suffocation in my chest" (*orhdeam' muja fugar zata*). Gizelino is reported to have incorporated these words in his mando. The only one we know where these words occur is the chorus of the third verse of the song *Dove rozeritso kollo* (*Utrike* 45), which is perhaps his.

Gizelino excels the other composers of the Mando in the qualities of *porzoll* (brightness) and *sontos* (joy). Yet the tone of his life was set by a bleak unhappiness and melancholy. His sad childhood had been traumatic, and in later life he saw frustration in love. In his moments of gloom (and even self-pity) his poetry confronted a grim void. Only once does he tell us of the causes of his unhappiness, in his *Foxalborit bountai amim* (*Villap* 17), with its finely contrasted antitheses and its sublime satire. One of his last mandos is the *Kakultty tsoiyai tumim muji* (*Villap* 16), a cry of pain. Aramita Barreto believes this to have been his very last work, but a Leopoldina Fernandes told us that, three months before his death, Gizelino had shown her another mando in the early stages of its composition, and was told that he had yet to finalize it. Leopoldina's memory did not retain the song, which is now sadly lost.

Gizelino died of influenza on 20 November 1931. He is said to have caught the disease from Nascimenta's young son Vicente (who died around 1998). As the composer lay dying, his sister Utílcia suggested that Nascimenta go to Morhgoum to carry the news to brother Genserico, but Gizelino refused to let her go, so that she could stay and nurse her sick child, Vicente (*tak' dan-nnaka, tage' cherhea' zor aila*, "do not send her, her boy has fever").

Torquato de Figueiredo (1876-1948)

Torquato was born of a branch of the family of the Figueiredos of Sankvall/Sancoale. He used to tell the following story about his ancestors. Rich and prosperous landlords, they were accustomed to go to church on horseback, unlike others of their kind who went in palanquins or on foot. They were Brahmins, and, by privilege, the color of their wives' ceremonial *torhop baz* conformed to that of the day's vestments. They displayed their arrogance by tying their horses under the church's choir loft at the entrance. The church reacted quickly; under instructions from the archbishop, the priests removed the Blessed Sacrament from the tabernacle, and left the edifice by the side door. Not long afterwards, a fire broke out in the building, the blaze consuming everything but the church's façade (which is all that is left of it today). Seeing this as a divine curse, the landlords left Sankvall; some of them migrated to Lotlli.

It is hard to verify the truth of this story, but the church was in fact burnt in 1834. Torquato was born 42 years after this event, on 26 September 1876, of Manuel Vicente de Figueiredo and Conceição Sobrinho. He was the youngest son, preceded by two brothers, Sérgio and Francisco Paulo. When he was between 7 and 10, his father died.

Torquato is reported to have gone to school on the Monte S. Sebastião at Lotlli. The chapel on that hill had been built no more than eight years before our composer was born, but the adjoining school itself was opened by Padre Evaristo de Figueiredo in 1893, when Torquato was 17. Among Padre Evaristo's assistants were the padres Inacinho da Costa and Lourenço de Figueiredo (who later became the examiner in philosophy of the students of the Liceu at Panaji/Ponnji/Panjim). The founder's brother, Padre Caetano José de Figueiredo, taught in the school until he was appointed professor at the Rachol Seminary; both there and elsewhere he acquired a name for being able to express complex theological ideas in simple language. Among Torquato's other instructors was a Santana de Figueiredo, probably his music teacher. We have been given to understand that a Padre Pedro Paulo Mota, 17 years Torquato's senior, may have been his Latin teacher. These men were qualified to give our young composer the best education that he could get anywhere in Goa. Another learned priest that he may have had contact with was the Konkani scholar Padre Francisco Xavier Araújo (1878-1949), almost his contemporary, whose diaries of everyday events in Lotlli (which we have unfortunately been unable to consult) may well have something to tell us about Torquato and life in Lotlli in those days.

On leaving school Torquato, like many other young men of his time, may have gone to the Rachol Seminary for further studies, and there had the opportunity to learn some plain-chant. In 1863, Archbishop Amorim Pessoa had reformed the institution's curriculum, which of course included plain-chant, and the Seminary had, for many decades afterwards, excelled in its rendering. Some of Torquato's melodies reflect the solemnity of Gregorian and other church music.

Sometime after he had finished his education, Torquato got a job as a private tutor - a post he held in three places at various periods in his life: in Bannali/Benaulim; at the house of a rich man named Saukar at Bori (opposite the river from Lotlli); and in Lotlli itself, where he taught music to the wealthy landlord António de Figueiredo's children. Most of his life was spent in his native village.

When in Bannali he appears to have fallen in love, as one of his good friends, Dr. Roque Menezes of Nuvem, who knew the composer from 1930 to 1943, believes. When questioned about it by the doctor, Torquato used to be evasive, smile and change the subject. At this time Torquato learnt to drink hard, in order to get over his frustration in love, the doctor says. Most of his best songs were composed when he was still a young man, in this sad period. Three of these are especially noteworthy; the first is the *Soglem mujem vido chintunum* (written before 1918), which is tragedy at its deepest in Goan Song. The second is the dialogue mando *Kedinch chintily'm naim re anvem*, and the third the profound *Adeus kortso vellu pauta*, where one feels, at its most intense, the pulse of Goan migration (the throb of which was felt in Goa from around 1890).

The passing of youth saw Torquato's pattern of life becoming fixed. He seems to have had no ambition. His everyday needs were met by the fees he got through coaching children privately, which he did in his own house, teaching them to read and write and preparing them for the *primeiro* and *segundo grao* of Portuguese elementary education. Artur Menezes, the eldest son of his musically most sensitive lay admirer, Roque Menezes, was one of his pupils.

Torquato was offered many jobs, but he turned them down. Some of these were bureaucratic, at Ponnji. An influential person, the uncle of the Maestro António de Figueiredo, invited him to become the choir-master of the church at Lotllli, which was mainly an honorary post, the honorarium not more than five rupees a year. But for Torquato neither the prestige (nor the money) was inducement enough.

However, he did accept the post of choir-master of the chapel in his ward, Devotti. His predecessor, one Aleixo Costa, had been expelled by the chaplain Padre Pedro Alcantara Lamartine de Quadros (known as Pad Pedrinh) for having written a mando lampooning him - which so infuriated the victim, that he slapped the choir-master. The new incumbent to the post was an exemplary successor, for he wrote a devout mando commemorating the setting up of the statue of the chapel's patroness, the Mãe de Deuṣ (Mother of God), which took place on 7 January 1903. Torquato always took charge of the singing during the novenas in that chapel, for no financial remuneration.

Though unwilling to be choir-master in the Lotlli church, he was still prominent in its services. He and his colleague, a Francisco Xavier Soares (the choir-master?) were often heard discussing aloud in church as to what numbers to sing at the services. One of our mando informants, Aramita Barreto, herself a gifted singer, who used to attend these services, says that she had seldom heard a voice in Goa better than Torquato's, and that for her the singing in the Lotlli church was also the best she had heard in any Goan church. The real conductor of the choir during these services was Torquato, and his own voice could manage the most complicated tremolos. Dr. Menezes describes the composer's voice as baritone and bass, melodious and "sweet", of a metallic timbre.

Torquato was often given charge of the Holy Week ceremonies, and of their many hymns, he was often asked to sing the *Stabat Mater*. Once he had a bad leg, but he still limped to church not to miss singing it, and his rendering that day is said to have been particularly moving. He must also have sung motets on such occasions, for he was once seen holding a sheet with the score of a motet, with the copy that his family possessed of the *Porje muje*, a Konkani translation of the motet *Popule meus*. He was himself a composer of motets, as well as of an *Ave maris stella*, several litanies and even some masses.

But church singing was not the main outlet for his musical talent. His was a deeply religious mind, which found fulfillment not in liturgical and devotional music, but in mandos of marriage and personal sorrow, when he approached these crucial moments of life with great seriousness, and not seldom, solemnity. Hearing a mando well sung gave him great satisfaction, but an unmusical rendering would make him turn his face upwards and roll his eyes in mock despair.

But he was not always humorlessly intolerant of bad singing. At the wedding of a daughter of "Muzg" Augusto at Morhgoum, Torquato asked Elizena Vaz, one of his friends and good interpreters, to accompany the bride in singing the marriage mando. The bride sang out of tune, but Torquato waited till she had finished the first verse. Then, signing Elizena to stop, he began himself to accompany the bride, imitating her style of singing. The bride was annoyed, surprisingly not with Torquato, but with Elizena, so much so that she never spoke to her after that.

Mandos are followed by dulpods, and singers would work themselves to frenzy by singing one dulpod after another, now quickening the pace, now slackening it, seeking by this to perplex, bewilder and exhaust other singers and the dancers. Once at a wedding of a man called Miguelinho (Ribeiro?) there was a competition between Saxttykars and other Goans to see who would tire last in a mando-and-dulpod sequence. With careful deliberation, Torquato tied a handkerchief round his neck and joined in the singing. It all began happily, but as first the minutes and then the hours went by, people began to give up, but not Torquato, who sang through the whole night and stopped long after the others had lapsed into an admiring silence. One of the dulpods he is said to have sung on this occasion was

> *Tsoi tsoi tsoi tsoi tsoinum - tsoinum tsoinum*
> *Tsoinum ol-lly' muje dolle*
> *Sanje matxe euxi zalea' polle.*

Torquato had his own throat tonics to help him in these *tours de force* of singing; one was ginger, a piece of which he always carried in his pocket. Elizena recalls how he would steal silently to her side to say that it helped if one kept one's head raised while singing the alto, and in its normal position when doing the tenor.

One of Torquato's greatest performances must have been on the occasion of Goa's greatest religious event, the exposition, in Velha Goa, of the body of Francis Xavier, the Apostle of the Orient. We know that he attended the exposition of 1900, when Arnaldo too was one of the pilgrims.

But what made Torquato renowned was his composing, though it took only a fraction of his time. After his first songs, produced under great personal stress, he handled most wedding mandos, but only when asked to. In the choice of words and arrangement of ideas, he would consult his friends, chiefly those directly involved in the wedding. In the *Suryan uzvarh fankarolo,* composed in 1940, he changed a word in the second verse at the suggestion of Roque Menezes. The relevant line of that verse was to have read *Nimann' desej tuj' tivatso,* but Roque suggested that he replace the word *desej,* which was Portuguese (*desejo*) with the more authentically Konkani *visvas.* These compositions were written on loose sheets of paper, some of which are in our possession, on notebooks for his music pupils (among whom was Maria Figueiredo e Mesquita), and on two songbooks, unfortunately lost.

The normal tempo of Torquato's life was calm. Passers-by used to see him stretched out on an easy chair on his veranda (*bollcaum*), wearing clean pyjamas, reciting his rosary, which he did at any odd time. As Roque Menezes says, Torquato had the look of an aristocrat, commanding respect. His favorite suit was of a white color, with the jacket buttoned at the neck. He was tall and passably good-looking, with a face "between square and oval," and of a light hue. Though he never married, women seem to have found him attractive. He had a firm step, and smoked a *virhi* - a cigarillo with the tobacco wrapped in a leaf instead of a sheet of paper.

Torquato showed no sign of wanting to acquire fame as a composer. All he wanted was to see his friends live tranquil and happy lives. He was a kind and trustworthy man, and his friendship was highly valued to those to whom it was given. He was not talkative, and when he did speak, it was about trite everyday things. He was never heard to boast or complain.

Whatever hidden frustrations Torquato may have had, they were quenched by his nine-day drinking bouts, ironically called his "novenas". In fact, he was an intermittent dipsomaniac. He would keep away from the bottle for three, four or even five months, and when, on some pretext on another, he would start to drink, it was usually only wine. He would then go on to the fierier Goan *fenny*, made from the toddy of the coconut palm. All of Torquato's cleanliness disappeared during this time; his aristocratic poise crumbled, leaving only a "dirty rag of humanity" in Dr. Menezes's words. The hapless musician then took to begging for money to buy his drinks, as one of his acquaintances, Rosarinho Noronha, told us. The doctor recalls a conversation (in Portuguese) between himself and the composer:

TORQUATO : *Ó meu amigo, quatro annás* (Friend, four annas, please!)
MENEZES : (no answer)
TORQUATO : *Dois annás!* (Two annas.)
MENEZES : Não tenho! (I do not have them.)
TORQUATO : *Um anná!* (One anna.)
MENEZES : *Vai embora, Torquato, não dou!* (Go away, Torquato, I won't give it to you.)

His second last novena, in September 1940, was very serious. His two doctor friends, Menezes and Melo, were with him during the crisis and fought to save his life. When they had brought him around, they felt that they had almost raised him from the dead. Before his last novena, which during the Carnival of 1948 (the last year of his life) he used to drink only on one day of the year - the feast of the chapel of Santa Cruz which stands on the dyke of the Lotlli lake.

From his seat in the veranda of his house, and during his walks through the village, his attendance at weddings, and his trips to the church, he seems to have observed the doings of his fellows carefully. He held conservative views, and was shocked when he found that the women of his village had begun to wear knee-high and décolleté dresses even in church. This seems to have been a fashion in Goa's capital town of Ponnji already in the 1820s, which was curbed by the fervent preaching of an Oratorian priest. Thus the phenomenon which so irritated Torquato was a sort of revival, an irritation which he gave vent to in his mando-dulpod *Kosli zali re odixi*. But, unlike Arnaldo, he seems to have left the much-maligned *beatinnys* alone. Like Arnaldo, however, he pilloried his quarrelsome and grasping villagers for displaying their love of intrigue and bickering in the course of the capital village event, the auctioning of the common agricultural land (*arrematasaum* or *launnim-paunnim*). He disliked both the Village Commune (*gaumponn* or *cumdade/ comunidade*) as an institution and the litigation (so dear to the Goans) that it encouraged. He used to say that it was wise not to meddle with either, because they destroyed a man ("*cumdadint anim demandam' och'nim - caba' zat' munis* "). He was also against Goans emigrating; how strongly he felt about this is reflected in his mando *Adeus*.

He must doubtless have read the local newspapers, for he wrote a long mando - his longest - on World War I. Only one manuscript (which we have been unable to consult) is said to record it. Torquato does not seem to have favored Portuguese rule in Goa, believing it better for the colony to have been administered by the British. And he was no ardent Indian nationalist either. His politics appears to have been one of indifference. He was heard to have said, *Lá se governe; façam como melhor entender* (Let them rule and do what they think best).

We know little of his last days. The wedding mando for Angela Mascarenhas, composed in 1947, was probably his last. One can sense the creative flame dying; indeed, it had been flaring palely since 1940. The great days of the Mando were over, and Torquato was a lone survivor of a stable age in a disintegrating Goa. He died on 1 August 1948 and was buried in the parish cemetery at Lotlli. Sometime afterwards, his bones were exhumed and thrown into a common pit.

Appendix 3

Alphabetical List of the Composers and Their Mandos

ANONYMOUS, Ek dis bagint aum gelolim (*Villap* 5)
ANONYMOUS, Maingeri paigeri (*Villap* 2)
ANONYMOUS, Zaite sukanum varholim, ANONYMOUS (*Villap* 3)
ARNALDO DE MENEZES, Ai, kitem anvem korchem (*Villap* 7)
ARNALDO DE MENEZES, Chintun furhar Deva muzo (The Adolfinian Trilogy, 3.*Villap* 10)
ARNALDO DE MENEZES, Motim' sopnnantum naxlolem (The Adolfinian Trilogy, 2. *Villap* 9)
ARNALDO DE MENEZES, Oromb nuim re y amcha Gointso (*Villap* 13)
ARNALDO DE MENEZES, Sintment varoily' e sonsrako (*Villap* 11)
ARNALDO DE MENEZES, Soglem vido mum re mujem (*Ekvott* 5)
ARNALDO DE MENEZES, Soglem vido mujem tsounum (*Villap* 12)
ARNALDO DE MENEZES, Tuzo mogu axlol' munnum (The Adolfinian Trilogy, 1. *Villap* 8)
AZAVEDO DINIZ, Tisri kunvori mum go tum (*Ekvott* 3)
CÉSAR-MENDES, Dony-tinim muinnem zale muj' moga (*Villap* 6)
DOMINGOS MASCARENHAS, Sarkeanum kituli tum nitolli (*Ekvott* 1)
FRANCISCO SARDINHA, Aji pasun Devachery patieunum (*Ekvott* 18)
GIZELINO REBELO, Chintun cabar korum' nuzo (*Villap* 15)
GIZELINO REBELO, Diso ekleponnantule (*Ekvott* 6)
GIZELINO REBELO, Foxalborit bountai y amim (*Villap* 17)
GIZELINO REBELO, Koslem vido mum re y amchem (*Villap* 14)
GIZELINO REBELO, Lanom burgeponnam sanum (*Ekvott* 7)

GIZELINO REBELO, Nirmit zaunum re Devachem (*Ekvott* 8)
GIZELINO REBELO, Sontos bogta re jivako (*Ekvott* 9)
GIZELINO REBELO, Surya sontosan udelo (*Ekvott* 10)
GIZELINO REBELO, Suryan uzvarhu dampilo (*Ekvott* 11)
GIZELINO REBELO, Kakultty tsoiyai tumim muji (*Villap* 16)
JOAQUIM MENEZES, Sodanch chintitalim y aum-um (*Ekvott* 17)
LUÍS MENEZES, Sonsar charich re disantso (*Villap* 1)
LUZITANO RODRIGUES, Soglem mujem vido chintunum (*Villap* 19)
MESTRE *JANTU*, Inocenti mujem vido (*Ekvott* 2)
PASCOAL NORONHA, Amcha gorchanche foxenum (*Ekvott* 16)
PASCOAL NORONHA, Paicha maincha moreantulim (*Ekvott* 15)
PAULO MILAGRES SILVA, Tsondrimm kupam' fankarolo (*Villap* 4)
ROQUE CORREIA-AFONSO, Bara tera vorsam zalim (*Ekvott* 4)
TORQUATO DE FIGUEIREDO, Derfente uzvarh fankarolo (*Ekvott* 12)
TORQUATO DE FIGUEIREDO, Soglem mujem vido chintunum (*Villap* 18)
TORQUATO DE FIGUEIREDO, Sontos bogta re jivako (*Ekvott* 13)
TORQUATO DE FIGUEIREDO, Suryan uzvarh fankarolo (*Ekvott* 14)
UTÍLCIA REBELO, Kity'm kon-n sanddun gel' re maka, (*Villap* 20)

Appendix 4

Alphabetical List of Mandos of **Ekvott** *and* **Villap**

Ai, kitem anvem korchem, ARNALDO DE MENEZES (*Villap* 7)
Aji pasun Devachery patieunum, FRANCISCO SARDINHA (*Ekvott* 18)
Amcha gorchanche foxenum, PASCOAL NORONHA (*Ekvott* 16)
Bara tera vorsam zalim, ROQUE CORREIA-AFONSO (*Ekvott* 4)
Chintun cabar korum' nuzo, GIZELINO REBELO (*Villap* 15)
Chintun furhar Deva muzo (The Adolfinian Trilogy, 3), ARNALDO DE MENEZES (*Villap* 10)
Derfente uzvarh fankarolo, TORQUATO DE FIGUEIREDO (*Ekvott* 12)
Diso ekleponnantule, GIZELINO REBELO (*Ekvott* 6)
Dony-tinim muinnem zale muj' moga, CÉSAR-MENDES (*Villap* 6)
Ek dis bagint aum gelolim, ANONYMOUS (*Villap* 5)
Foxalborit bountai y amim, GIZELINO REBELO (*Villap* 17)
Inocenti mujem vido, MESTRE *JANTU* (*Ekvott* 2)
Kakultty tsoiyai tumim muji, GIZELINO REBELO (*Villap* 16)
Kity'm kon-n sanddun gel' re maka, UTÍLCIA REBELO (*Villap* 20)
Koslem vido mum re y amchem, GIZELINO REBELO (*Villap* 14)
Lanom burgeponnam sanum, GIZELINO REBELO (*Ekvott* 7)
Maingeri paigeri, ANONYMOUS (*Villap* 2)
Motim' sopnnantum naxlolem (The Adolfinian Trilogy, 2), ARNALDO DE MENEZES (*Villap* 9)
Nirmit zaunum re Devachem, GIZELINO REBELO (*Ekvott* 8)
Oromb nuim re y amcha Gointso, ARNALDO DE MENEZES (*Villap* 13)
Paicha maincha moreantulim, PASCOAL NORONHA (*Ekvott* 15)
Sarkeanum kituli tum nitolli, DOMINGOS MASCARENHAS (*Ekvott* 1)
Sintment varoily' e sonsrako, ARNALDO DE MENEZES (*Villap* 11)
Sodanch chintitalim y aum-um, JOAQUIM MENEZES (*Ekvott* 17)

INDEX TO CHAPTER 1, PROLOGUE